Google
AdWords that work

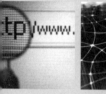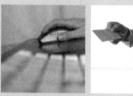

Jo, thank you ;)

Google

AdWords that work

The 7 secrets for cashing in with the
world's no. 1 search engine

Jon Smith

CAREFUL NOW

There are both good and bad sources of information available on the Internet, in the telephone directory, and advertised on bad photocopies for 20 pence a week in the local newsagents. The Internet, especially, is a constantly changing phenomenon and therefore good (and bad) sites are forever popping up and dropping off. Web addresses change, so if a link doesn't work, be sure to use Google (funnily enough) to try to find its new home, or a similar service offered by another firm or individual. You should have an up-to-date virus checker installed before you visit new sites and download anything whatsoever, and you should be aware that new applications may squabble and bicker over *who's the daddy* – they might not work because of other things you have installed on your machine. We're very sorry about all this and wish it was a better world, but it's the only one we have. We believe in taking it on the chin like grown ups and expect you to do the same. We love you dearly but if it all goes kumquat shaped then you're on your own; we take no liability. See it as an adventure.

First published in 2009 by
The Infinite Ideas Company Limited
36 St Giles
Oxford, OX1 3LD
United Kingdom
www.infideas.com

A CIP catalogue record for this book is available from the British Library

ISBN 978-1-905940-98-1

Brand and product names are trademarks or registered trademarks of their respective owners.

Designed and typeset by Baseline Arts Ltd, Oxford
Cover designed by Cylinder
Printed in India

Contents

Introduction

Google is massive – not just in terms of the
company's fiscal wealth but also in terms of its
power and influence on the web. It is the most searched
engine in the western world and is not doing too badly
everywhere else on the planet either[1].

You know something's big when a company name becomes
a verb – in the UK we still 'hoover' a room with a vacuum
cleaner manufactured by Dyson. Today, I 'google' job
candidates before interview and many of my readers 'google'
me to check whether or not what I say works. To Google *is*
to search. It is now so influential that if you've got an online
business and you want it to succeed you simply have to sit
up and pay attention.

1. At time of writing, Google's share of the UK search market was 74.9% and its
share of the US market was 49.7%. Source:
www.hitwise.co.uk/datacenter/searchengineanalysis.php

This book is intended for website owners, marketing managers, project managers and anyone interested in promoting their website effectively. It is also for the non-techie who wants to be involved – it will show you how to research, prepare and run your own AdWords campaign as well as giving you the tools and the confidence to be able to explain to other team members, third-party suppliers, and anyone else you care to talk to, what it is you want them to do for you.

In *Get Into Bed With Google: top ranking search optimisation techniques*, I explained to readers the importance of improving your website's natural, or organic, listing and explored 52 proven techniques for rising up the rankings. The techniques work but with the best will in the world they don't happen overnight – it took me a few years of patience and constant tweaking to get the number 1 spot for the keyword 'Jon Smith'.... The web is constantly evolving; new websites pop up, old ones drop off. As marketing professionals we understand the importance of brand awareness, exposure and 'getting our name known and out there' – and that's where Google AdWords can come in. Remember, though, that Google AdWords is not a replacement for investing in optimising your site; it should work hand in hand with your search engine optimisation strategy.

An effective Google AdWords campaign is a necessity if you take your business seriously and you want everybody else to do the same. Firstly, AdWords offers the chance to build brand awareness cheaply and effectively. Your short- to medium-term plan may well be to improve your natural listing on Google and other search engines, but you don't want to be sitting idle while this process is taking place – AdWords gets you in the search public's eye here and now. If your campaign's well thought out and well managed, and you follow the advice in this book, then you're only going to be paying when real prospects click through to a specific page, product or area of your site – and there's a high probability that they are going to convert into customers. Secondly, AdWords can offer you a real chance of getting big, fast. This isn't about throwing a limitless budget at Google and seeing what happens, with your fingers crossed that something will stick; quite simply, through a systematic and prepared campaign, you can fairly easily grow from obscurity to perceived market leader in less than six months – now how's that for a brilliant return on investment?

AdWords is a new breed of online advertising that adheres to the fundamental rules of marketing, but with its own unique twist – Google won't reveal what works and what doesn't because it would only lead to users abusing the system, so they keep quiet. There is no official guide to Google AdWords, but I trust you will find this 'unofficial' guide to be clear, concise and effective. I've tested these techniques on a number of sites, both high profile and some more obscure, and I assure you they work – and they work well.

Ready to get started? Then let me take your hand (metaphorically speaking, of course!) ...

1

AdWords – what's it all about?

In the beginning ...

My professional online marketing career began in 1998. Although the Internet as a medium for exchanging information was already established, certainly among techies and academics, the whole concept of e-commerce and the marketing machine that would go behind promoting and commercialising online business was still very much in its infancy.

As a team of about thirty individuals, we were about to unleash Amazon.co.uk onto the great British public. Not only were we trying to build brand awareness of a new business, but we were also trying to do it through a medium most of our potential customers were unaware of and, worse, afraid of! We not only had to educate people about our new exciting book store, but we also had to assure people that online ordering was safe, secure and reliable. All things considered, we did a pretty good job of it, but it's fair to say a lot of our efforts were hit and miss, and a lot can be attributed to luck, being in the right place at the right time and taking a few risks that really paid off.

Online marketing was new; online marketing was an unknown; but mainly ... online marketing was a mess. Advertisers had no idea how much to pay and how best to track performance, and the portals and high-traffic sites offering advertising space had no real idea how much their space was worth. Some incredible amounts of money changed hands over the following years and then, as is well documented, the entire Internet industry was forced to face up to the realities of economics. The dot-com bubble burst – billions of pounds and dollars were simply gone. There were a few survivors, Amazon being one of them, but there were lots and lots of losers, some of them high profile but many more who hadn't even enjoyed a few months of paper success.

Online marketing and advertising didn't cause the dot-com boom, but it did have a part to play in the super-high valuations being placed on dot-com companies at the time. When the shaky foundations of over-valued and poorly planned multi-billion dollar companies gave way, it all came tumbling down.

The truth was out: to make an online business successful you still needed to adhere to the basic rules of good old-fashioned bricks and mortar businesses. This realisation forced a re-think in terms of how to market websites. Advertisers were no longer prepared to just outbid their rivals and throw piles of cash away on banner ads, skyscrapers and rotating animated GIFs – online advertising needed to get clever. Online marketing and advertising needed to follow the same rules as its offline cousin – ROI (return on investment) became king. The hedonistic days of paying a flat fee or rental for a prime 'real estate' position for your banner advert had gone, as had the short-lived fad of *cost per thousand* (paying a site every time it served your advert to one thousand visitors, whether or not the advert resulted in an attributable sale).

It all changed when Google came along with AdWords. In fairness, AdWords, when it was first launched in 2002, was a bit ropey and was really just a rehash of what organisations like Overture were also trying to do at the time. However, Google did it in a slicker and smarter way. Google listened to what its users (read: advertisers; read: paymasters) wanted and implemented those ideas. Google quickly became the market leader in paid-for placement or *search advertising* and no one has knocked the company off its perch yet.

How important is Google AdWords to your business? Very important indeed. In fact, I'll even go as far to say that you are not fully utilising the potential of your online business *unless* you are using Google AdWords.

You've changed your tune - what about organic listings?

In *Get Into Bed With Google: top ranking search optimisation techniques*, Google AdWords is barely mentioned – and with good reason; the book's aim is to focus your efforts on optimising your site so that it is easily found and highly ranked within the natural or organic search results of Google and other search engines. But that's not to say that AdWords wasn't important then – far from it! 'Search engine optimisation' (SEO) and 'search advertising' are two different beasts and work completely independently of each other. You can have a strong SEO campaign and a weak AdWords campaign, or visa versa, but what's going to get potential consumers clicking on links, visiting your site and becoming customers of your services or products? By having a strong presence in both, customers need to be able to find you by natural search *and* by search advertising – it's their choice, it's their web session and it's *your* job to ensure that your website is there no matter what route the user takes. This book focuses on Google AdWords, so you'll need to put your hand in your pocket again and buy *Get Into Bed With Google* if you're looking for SEO advice!

Yes, but if you had to choose one, would it be Google organic or Google AdWords?

They're different! Stop comparing! OK, here's my philosophy on this. I'm a strong believer in making the websites I'm involved in easy to find. That means optimising your pages so that they can rank highly in natural search *and* paying for search advertising. Firstly, the way I look at it, it's better to take up two (or more!) of the slots available on page 1 of the search results than one – and that means paying for at least one of those listings through

AdWords. Secondly, SEO is not an exact science. Google and the other search engines are forever modifying their algorithms to keep website owners guessing: just as you achieve the exalted number 1 slot for your favourite keyword, it all changes and you find yourself banished to the depths of page 15 and it all starts again. Because no money changes hands, you're not in control and nor can you shout at anyone when things go wrong. With Google AdWords, you get what you pay for. And it's the act of paying for this service that means that there is a science to it. There has to be, otherwise, put simply, if it wasn't working for companies (and working effectively) then they would stop using the service. Is Google seeing a rise or fall in take-up and expenditure on its AdWords programme? Well, you've just bought this book, what do you think?

Google's intent

If you still need convincing about whether you can go it 'solo' by just banking on your current search results ranking without the added benefit and safety net of AdWords, then think about this ...

Google's success is in part due to its refreshingly sparse look and feel. This 'clutter-free' approach was and still is an oasis of calm in what is a very busy online landscape. Google is a search engine and its main feature – nay its *raison d'être* – is the search box, with cursor flashing, awaiting your query. Google has never sold space on its homepage to advertisers. Advertising and commercial promotion is not Google's focus; information is. Google offers as many, if not more, tools and applications than any of the leading portal sites, yet the homepage remains pretty much as bare as it did way back in 1998 – the aim then and now is to offer users an effective search engine. Where the large portals of the late 1990s and early 2000s went wrong was to cram the homepage with links to every service and feature and confuse this with excessive amounts of third-party advertising. Why? Because that's how they made money. Google's primary job, if you like, is to return accurate responses to user queries – the priority is to provide users with information about the word or phrase queried. By nature, this means that websites that provide information will always rank higher than profit-driven sites (i.e. commercial or e-commerce sites). Although there are techniques you can employ to buck the trend, you will always be playing second fiddle to informational sites. Therefore, if you truly accept what Google's main purpose is, it doesn't take a quantum leap to realise that, since there is a paid-for search advertising facility available through Google, you can rest assured that it's there for a reason. Yes, of course, Google is a business and wants to make money, but it can do that through AdWords whilst still ensuring that users come back again and again because the Google Search works so well. Google's purpose is to offer users unbiased results to their queries. Its algorithm (despite constantly changing) will thus always prefer an informational website over a commercial one. Therefore, if you've got something to sell, Google is basically insisting that you pay to advertise your site, and in return Google will send you interested, relevant and 'targeted' users who have a genuine interest in your product or service. You pay, they deliver.

No inbound links, no joy...

A critical component of search engine optimisation has always been links. A few years ago this caused a craze, with every web owner flooding their sites with links to other websites in return for reciprocal links from those other websites. Web owners abused the system and Google threw its toys out of the pram. The *zeitgeist* now is to favour *inbound links* – i.e. lots of other websites linking to you, thus giving you 'authority' status in the eyes of Google (as long as you do not reciprocate those links). A site that enjoys lots of inbound links tends to enjoy a very high ranking on Google search. So, it could be argued that the key to SEO is thousands of inbound links ... and herein lies the problem. Who is going to want to link to you? If your pages are content rich, unbiased, informational and informative, you stand a fighting chance but you're looking at promoting your website through AdWords because you run a business – and therefore your website is commercial by definition. Yes, I'm sure you've got great copy, great product or service descriptions, great images and your sales messages are world-beating, but you'll never be 'content rich' in the true sense and therefore very few websites are going to want to link to you. Enter AdWords, the great leveller. With AdWords it doesn't matter if you don't have any inbound links and it doesn't matter if Google sees your site as authoritative or not – if you get your campaign right, you'll be displayed on page 1 every time.

When's a good time to start an AdWords campaign?

Now! Seriously, if your site is live, it's time to start your campaign as soon as possible; you need to be utilising AdWords immediately (although, obviously, give this book a quick once-over first). Why the rush? Well, for starters, AdWords really works and, depending on your industry, it can work for you with little to medium investment. The reason AdWords is so effective is that every aspect of your campaign is measurable and, in terms of cost per new customer, you'd be hard pushed to find anything else that works out so affordable and offers a global reach twenty-four hours a day, seven days a week. On top of that, the major reason you need to start your AdWords campaign *now* is that it's still to catch on. Seriously, despite the fact that it is almost seven years old, a lot of companies are still to (a) realise it's there and (b) realise its full potential. Believe it or not, you're still one of the early adopters and, if your budget is quite tight, you can still get an effective campaign operational for very little outlay. Inevitably this will all change when your competition decides to focus a bit more effort on search advertising – but, before then, get big, fast and blow them out of the water!

Controlling what users see

AdWords puts you back in the driving seat. You might have spent hours optimising your pages but that's no guarantee that Google will index each page as highly as you would like. Your website may not rank at all or, worse, sometimes the wrong pages are ranking highly.

For the search term *Monte Cristo Musical*, I have positions 1, 2, 3 and 6 of the natural listings. I'm pretty pleased about that. However, the listing on position three quotes the Flash source file behind the site. It's not a huge problem, because the link takes users to the website I want them to visit, but Google is displaying some of the 'code' behind the site:

[FLASH] <font face="Tahoma" size="10" color="#e5e1ba ...
File Format: Shockwave Flash
  </font> **MONTE CRISTO** by Jon Smith & Leon Parris Running Time: 2:21 **MONTE CRISTO** - THE **MUSICAL** COMPLETED, MAY 2007. ... www.**montecristothemusical**.com/sources.swf - Similar pages - Note this

This is not the sales message I created; this is not the 'look' I want for my listing; and it's highly unlikely that anyone would want to click through to find out more. Thankfully, this search result is sandwiched between search results that utilise the <title> and <description> I wrote and I still get the visitor. But what if this were my only search result? I wouldn't have a visitor. And this is where AdWords really helps: you can dictate the message, the positioning, how often the advert is served, to which locations and, depending on your budget, how many people can both see and click through to your page – and it's your control over the destination page that is critical. If you're an online store selling teapots and speciality teas and you want to promote your Darjeeling range, then you can do just that, bringing users right to where you want them rather than your generic homepage, or, in the case above, to a page of Google's own choosing!

You stroke my back ...

This really is conjecture – and certainly when I asked Google customer support, they categorically denied it – but I do believe having a long campaign history with Google has benefits. It's quite simple, really: Google is a business and will want to encourage proven advertisers. If you have a history with Google and your campaigns have a good click-through rate, I can't help feeling you are offered slightly cheaper bids for higher positions. I can't prove it because I haven't run exactly the same campaign from two different accounts.

Whether it's true or not, the sooner you're up and running (and spending money) with Google, the better it is. Yes, some of your competitors will always have a longer track record than you – that's life. But even if you open your first Google AdWords campaign today, you're still an early adopter in the grand scheme of things. Think of the many hundreds of thousands if not millions of advertisers who are still to utilise AdWords. You'll always have a longer campaign history than them.

2

Defining your strategy

To fully harness the potential of Google AdWords, it's of paramount importance to fully understand what Google AdWords is, how it works, and how you can make it work for you and your online business. You may have dabbled with AdWords already and enjoyed some success or suffered abject failure. You may have been using AdWords for years and you're just reading this book to find a couple of hints and tips to improve on your current campaigns. Whatever your background with AdWords, it never hurts to take a breather, refresh yourself and 'go back to basics' – not least because Google is always changing and we all run the risk of falling into a rut with our behaviour and thought processes, which means we can often overlook some of the simple ways to improve our campaigns.

Google AdWords in a nutshell

AdWords is advertising, pure and simple. Google knows it's got a search engine that works and that users trust. Of the many millions of searches that take place on Google every single day, some of them will be for a word or phrase (*keyword*) that relates to the product or service that your website offers. Users see the search results to that keyword query in list format and from there they may or may not click on a link to a website. If you are lucky, there is a link to your website on page 1 of those search results, but for many of us this isn't the case. While there is a lot that can be done in terms of search engine optimisation, this might take a while to come into effect, and if it's a particularly busy and competitive market, we might never see our site ranked on the first page. So what are you to do? Give up?

No. AdWords allows you the opportunity to place an advert in front of Google users searching for one of your keywords, with immediate effect. Those users may be searching for that word or phrase for a whole host of reasons – not everyone is shopping 24/7 (although, as optimistic marketing types, we really wish they were). There will be users who search for *Jimmy Choo shoes* but who don't actually want to buy them, ever – e.g. me! I searched for them to find out what all the fuss was about, and, to be honest, I still don't understand. But then again, I'm a bloke and no matter how deeply in touch I am with my feminine side, I'll never wear heels, or spend more than about sixty notes on a pair of shoes for me or anyone else! Multiply this scenario across the day and it's apparent that most users are primarily searching for information, not for where they are going to spend their hard-earned cash next. However, some of those users are looking to buy, and, even though you might have only set up your website this morning, you can conceivably be listed on page 1 of the search results tonight if you want.

Let's say you've decided to retail garden gnomes. You've got a brand new website but, with no track record, no brand awareness and with no links, you're not regarded as an authority. You've just received your first consignment of garden gnomes from a supplier in Malaysia and you're ready to go. First AdWord campaign written in the morning, turn it on at lunchtime and bang! – there you are, top of the pile on page 1 that afternoon. And what's so great about AdWords is that it's entirely set up to only cost you money when it's working for you. All those users who are searching for images of garden gnomes just for something to do on a rainy day aren't costing you money – they'll see your advert, ignore it and click on the link to a garden gnome fan site or similar. But for the users who do want to buy garden gnomes, the likelihood is that they're going to be more open to reading and processing sales messages. They're keen to buy and your slickly written advert is just the tonic … they click, it costs you cash, but then they've found your site and will hopefully go on to become one of your first customers (not bad considering you only turned on AdWords a few hours ago).

AdWords works because it is so unobtrusive – obvious to those on the lookout for what it is you sell or do, and yet just part of the background for those users who are intent on something else – and the best bit is you are only paying for it when it's working for you. Not only has an advertiser never before had so much control over where, when and how an advert is displayed, but also the depth and breadth of the data you can receive on the advert's effectiveness (or not, as the case may be) is staggering. Google AdWords is your friend.

Getting results with Google AdWords – abridged

There are, of course, exceptions to the rule and other factors that must be considered, which we'll explore throughout this book, but generally speaking the more you are prepared to bid for a customer's click on your ad (in comparison to your competition), the higher up the list your ad appears. Other factors, of course, come into play, such as relevancy, but as a baseline AdWords is driven by how much you're prepared to pay Google per click, and how much other advertisers are prepared to pay for the same keyword. Money talks. Now the clever thing about AdWords is that Google does not value the depth of your wallet over all else. Your *ad rank* is also decided by how effective your ad is.

Now, assuming your advert is then ranked somewhere within the top six, hopefully you'll begin to receive *click-throughs*. The rate of click-throughs you receive in comparison to how many times the ad was shown (impressions) is represented as a click-through rate (CTR). This is expressed as a percentage figure. If your ad does not receive enough click-throughs (approximately one for every 200 impressions), Google will reduce how often it shows the ad. If the ad continues to fail, Google will disable it because it's not working for either of you.

I'm loath to write what a good CTR is, or what CTR you should be aiming for, because it depends on so many factors, not least how much you're paying per click and, should that click-through result in a user buying a product or a service from you, how much you charge for your product or service and how much of that is profit. So, I will leave you to decide for yourself what a good CTR is, and what a good conversion rate is, because it is particular to your own unique business.

The good news is, although you might have to bid high to get your new ad campaign established at first, if you have created an effective ad that attracts users and therefore results in click-throughs, Google will regard your ad well. Google rewards ads that work and will begin to lower the cost-per-click price of your ad – so, each click will begin to cost you less while you continue to maintain your high position. The more successful your Ad, the cheaper each click-through becomes, so you in turn get more clicks for your money. Assuming these click-throughs convert into customers, you'll have even more money to spend on AdWords, and the cycle continues. If only everything worked as smoothly as this! Unfortunately, there will be other advertisers competing for the same keywords, with similar ads all looking to jostle you for your position. This makes AdWords a constantly changing landscape and it is imperative you keep your eye on the ball.

Now, as a high CTR is one of the determining factors contributing to your ad's quality score, and thus positioning (and, therefore, the success of your ad campaign), it should be clear to see why writing that 'killer' ad is paramount. It is the ad copy that will attract users to click on your ad and it is the ad copy that will make your ad stand out from the other ads listed for that keyword. Every ad starts with a headline. A poor headline – or, worse, a headline that becomes part of the generic 'noise' on the page – is going to fail to attract clicks and, although non-clicks aren't costing you money, they're not making you money either.

Sadly it's not as easy as creating a winning ad and then sitting back and counting your millions. Oh no. You see, your competitors can see what your ad looks like, and if it's perceived to be more successful than theirs, then they're going to modify and improve their ad. These competitor alterations will affect your CTR and in turn you'll need to modify and improve yours to stay ahead of the game. You should know now that embarking on an AdWords campaign can reap rewards, but it is time consuming and involves real work. If you're not prepared to work at it, then it's probably best to stop before your start and put an ad in the Yellow Pages instead.

Still with me? Great. Well, let's explore some of this in a bit more detail ...

Setting up your 'campaign'

There's little point in me repeating what is freely available within the extensive 'Help' and 'Info' pages available on the Google website. What I will do, though, is expand on the areas where new users seem to have problems when first trying to navigate their way around setting up their first campaigns.

An important variable you will need to decide on at campaign level is the *networks* on which your ads will be shown. The good news is you can edit your choices at a later date, depending on whether you want to expand or reduce your exposure. These are the choices:

■ *Google Search* – this is pretty self-explanatory: the 'Google Search' page. When a user enters a keyword or phrase into Google's search box, Google displays the results on a 'search results' page. Now, on which Google search results page your ad will be displayed and in which position will be determined by the keywords you have chosen and the amount you have bid per click, plus a whole host of other determining factors explained later.

■ *Search Network* – is the generic term for Google's recognised partners. This list of partners will change over time, but they are trusted sites with which Google has a corporate relationship. Examples include AOL and Ask.com. So, if you decide to advertise on the Search Network, chances are your ads will show to users searching on partner websites other than Google. Bear in mind that although Google is big, 20% of web searches in the UK are taking place on search engines other than Google. That's one in five searches. Displaying your ads on the Search Network is a simple way to expand your exposure to non-Google users without having to set up numerous ad campaigns with numerous separate search engines.

- **Content Network** – the official info page from Google explains that the Content Network 'comprises hundreds of thousands of high-quality websites, news pages and blogs that partner with Google to display targeted AdWords ads'. The info page shows the branding of Channel 4, The Times Online, Capital FM and Vogue.com as example network partners. It is indeed true that there are a number of 'authority' websites, with good content and high traffic, who are signed up as Content Network partners, but for every one of these recognisable websites, there must be one hundred thousand micro-sites trying to get in on the action – essentially any monkey with a website or a blog who's trying to make 'millions' through running Google AdSense.

As you've probably guessed, I'm not a fan of the Content Network. I would love to be persuaded otherwise, but for me it has never worked. I find I don't get the click-throughs and, when I do, they don't convert. This could of course just be the industries and specific websites I've been promoting through AdWords, but I remain unconvinced. Certainly give it a go, but I strongly recommend turning Content Network off when you first launch a new campaign, for the simple reason that there are so many variables affecting your AdWords campaign and you need to try to remain in control of as much as possible. Being able to measure your CTR is one such variable. If everything is working well through Google Search, then feel free to expand across the Google Network. You'll be able to track very quickly whether the inclusion of your ads on the network is helping or hindering your performance.

If you do feel that Search Network and Content Network are something that you'd like to pursue, please go ahead, but I urge you to set up a separate campaign to manage your ads: one for Google Search, one for Content Network and one for Search

Network. You need to keep the CTRs separate so that it is quite clear what is working for you and where – in terms of understanding your ROI, with a separate campaign you'll be able to make a direct correlation between cost of advertising and sales as a direct result, without having to decipher the figures.

The beauty of doing separate campaigns is that it is also easier to manage your bids – which may differ wildly depending on the ad's destination. I've found the click-throughs from Content Network to be particularly haphazard and those users to be non-committal and therefore I'm far less willing to bid at the higher end of the scale. Without doubt, the best 'quality' of users are those generated through Google Search, so this should always be your major focus (unless real sales data prove that your ads and business buck the trend and work a treat through the Content Network or Search Network).

In defence of the Content Network, one of its strongest plus points is, depending on the partner site, the ability to display *image ads* and even *video ads*. I'll address video ads at the end of chapter 7 because I think some very exciting things are about to happen with Google AdWords and the embracing of video ads, and certainly the use of Image Ads, which are going to be of significant benefit to certain industries – not least those whose business is images and related commerce.

Make sense to AdSense

Those of you who wish to follow the path of advertising via Google's Content Network should bear in mind the types of sites that run Google AdSense. Although there are exceptions to the rule, more often than not these are sites that don't sell products or services themselves and therefore the revenue they receive from serving AdSense ads and other advertising represents their entire income stream. Generally they are content providers. It is therefore likely that the ads will be placed in a prominent position (high up on the page) – the trick is to make your ad fit in with the surrounding site. It won't always be the case, but many of the sites running AdSense are forum, portal or special interest sites, focused or concerned with a specific issue – e.g. www.writers.net, a website for existing and aspiring writers, runs AdSense. To encourage users to click on my ad from a Content Network page rather than a Google Search result page is going to require a slightly different approach to make my ad fit in.

Research the sites and choose which ones you wish to appear on rather than trying to cast your net wide – if you know where you're going to be, you can tailor your ads to speak to that specific audience who are going to be more likely to click on a specific ad tailored for them rather than a generic ad that's just fishing for clicks. Once you have a few weeks of activity clocked up, the reporting tool will show at a glance which sites you're appearing on and the conversion tracker will confirm if the impressions are converting to click-throughs for you. Remove yourself from the deadwood and improve the ads on your revised list of sites.

Daily budget

Please note that this is the budget you are prepared to spend per day, not how much you are prepared to spend per click. The bigger your budget the longer it will take for you to spend it and therefore the more impressions your ad will receive, which in turn increases the chances of users clicking through. Your budget is only spent when a user clicks on your Ad, not how many times your ad is shown (this is the number of impressions). Google will determine, based on its own algorithm, how often to show your ad based on (a) your total budget and (b) the price you are prepared to pay per click.

Let's say that you have a budget of £10 per day. Just to keep the numbers nice and simple, you are bidding £0.10 per click for the keyword 'garden gnome'. Again, to keep things simple, this is the only keyword you are bidding on and you only have one ad. So Google's algorithm will determine (based on a number of factors that include the previous performance of your ads and the performance of your competitor's ads) that on average your ad is clicked on five times for every one hundred times it is shown. Or, in the terminology you're beginning to familiarise yourself with, your ad gets a click-through rate of 5%. Therefore, over the course of a day if your ad is served to 2,000 users then at a CTR of 5% you can expect 100 of them to click through to your site. Now, your own website stats should be able to tell you what your conversion ratio is (i.e. the number of visitors to your website against the number who complete a purchase). Let's say you enjoy a conversion of 5% (i.e. for every one hundred visitors to your site, five of them purchase something). Let's also say that the average spend on your site is £25. You can quickly assess that your AdWords campaign cost you £10 for that day and resulted in sales of £125. If this were your business you'd be pretty happy with that return on investment and would probably look to double your AdWords spend to see if the trend in sales also doubled. Likewise, if you found that your budget of £10 was resulting in only one or even no sales, you'd quickly want to alter your ad and/or your destination URL. Otherwise you'd find yourself quickly out of pocket.

The hardest thing to decide about your daily budget is what figure to put on it? There is no 'one size fits all' answer. On one hand, you don't want to over-commit cash on unproven ads for keywords you have not worked with before. If the ads are getting click-throughs but those click-throughs aren't converting into customers then you're going to be getting through your daily budget quickly with little or no reward. Conversely, if you don't invest enough, especially in the first weeks and months, your ads may not be served up enough to give you a clear indication of what the interest is, or if your ads are working.

Thankfully, Google will suggest, based on the keywords you have selected, a recommended daily budget. This figure may be tonnes higher than you are prepared to spend; it might be only slightly higher; or it might even be lower than the figure you had in mind. The important thing, certainly for the initial two weeks when you are building up your data, is to try to spend as close to the recommended budget as you can. This figure really isn't Google trying to exploit your account for all it is worth; it's based on an algorithm of what activity has been like for ads using those keywords in the past. Google will have a good idea of your potential CTR and the budget will reflect a realistic amount of click-throughs so that both you and Google can benefit from a long and fruitful relationship. It could be that after two weeks you feel the budget needs to be reduced or increased – at least after two weeks you have some real data to help you make that decision, as opposed to just making an educated guess.

Delivery method

This determines at which time and frequency over a 24-hour period your ad is shown. If you're starting a campaign for the first time, I recommend choosing 'Standard', but there may be reason to select 'Accelerated'.

- ■ *Standard: show ads evenly over time* – the default setting. Google will determine, based on your daily budget, how often it needs to show your ad for there to be enough clicks to reach your daily budget. This is not an exact science and therefore you might not receive enough clicks that day to exhaust your budget. However, your ad will be shown throughout the entire 24-hour period, thus giving users the opportunity to see your ad whether they are searching Google during the day or night.

- ■ *Accelerated: show ads as quickly as possible* – choose this option if you are determined to spend your budget each day. Google will display your ad more often, with the intention that the budget is fully utilised. Once the daily budget has been exhausted, the ad will be removed until the next day. There is no guarantee that the budget will be spent because, of course, users have to click on the ad for the charge to be made.

Personally, I have always used Standard as it gives the ad a fair chance of catching users throughout any given day. I have met a number of heavy AdWords advertisers who always start new campaigns with Accelerated – their thinking being that they will get essential performance data about their ads quicker. If they have chosen Accelerated and they're not getting through their budget, then they know that there's something wrong with the ad message and will immediately make changes. Conversely, if their budget is being used up within a couple of hours, then they're not getting any more impressions for the rest of the day. This, after checking that those users that have clicked through have become prospects by signing up for something or customers by buying something, quickly points to the need to increase the daily budget to get more users. Similarly, if the users are all coming through fast and furious but not becoming prospects or customers, then both the ad and the destination URL need to be looked at and optimised.

Target audiences

Languages: This is simply a way to tell Google which language/s your ads are written in and therefore who best to serve them to. It really is a waste of time to have a campaign entirely in English and then select Russian even if you are selling Russian products or products that are of interest to Russian speakers. Use Locations to determine which country the ad is served to; Languages is for languages.

Locations: This is the country in which your potential customer lives. Now, I'm guessing most of you reading this book will want to choose the UK as a geographic location to begin with, so in this case your ad will be shown to users who search www.google.co.uk. If you added Spain as a location, then the ad would also be served to users searching on www.google.es and so on. Obviously as marketers and optimists we think people in every country around the world want to buy our products or benefit from our services, but you'll be wasting time and money serving your ads to the wrong sort of user. Although impressions don't cost you anything per se, they do have an effect on the performance of your ad in terms of your click-through rate and therefore your ad's viability and longevity.

When running a company called Toytopia, I was convinced there were thousands of British ex-pats living in Spain who would love to buy gifts for their loved ones back in the UK through a UK-based website and so I started an AdWords campaign that focused on the location of Spain with the ads written in English. It didn't work. Instead I focused my efforts solely on the UK and Ireland and later, once the site was translated into Spanish, I added Spain as a location again (along with a .es micro-site tailored to the ex-pats) and this time it did work.

Don't try to scattergun your marketing – keep it limited to your core audience/s and expand once you've proven your campaign works in one or a handful of locations.

Keyword bidding

The most important factor in this relationship for both you and Google, is the money. Google wants to maximise its revenue, and you want to keep your campaign costs to a minimum. Google, in my opinion, play it pretty fair – the cost of your campaign basically comes down to supply and demand on the keywords you are interested in.

If it's really niche and only a few other advertisers are bidding on that keyword, you're going to be enjoying a low cost per click. If, however, there are already a lot of other advertisers all wanting to attract clicks for the same keyword, then your Google AdWords campaign is going to be a whole lot more expensive. Google gives you the tools to experiment with your pricing and with the daily or monthly cap on spending your campaign can't get out of control. If your ad works, Google will reward you with a lower average cost per click, but only you will know if it's working. You might be a specialist software reseller and your keyword might be costing £10 per click, but if you are making £2,000 per sale it's a reasonable cost – but not so if you're only making £20 per sale.

Manual (or Maximum) bidding is the most common choice, as it gives you the most control over your bidding, especially if you have numerous campaigns and groups that you may want to work in different ways (i.e. an ad Group that you are deliberately bidding low on to test the waters, or because you find you get a better CTR when displayed at position 3 or 4, rather than position 1). It is important to note that the amount you enter as your bid is the *most* you are willing to pay per click and not necessarily what you will pay – that will depend on what other advertisers are paying and the performance of your ads. Only bid what you can afford!

Cost per acquisition bid is a handy little feature that was introduced recently to complement Google's 'Conversion Optimiser' tool. If you grant access to Google to monitor your users' behaviour from click-through to (hopefully) purchase or sign up, then this style of bidding may appeal. The idea is that you bid how much you are willing to pay for a conversion as opposed to a click-through. For all businesses, it is converting a user into a customer that is the true indicator of whether your AdWord campaign is working – click-throughs are worthless unless they end up as sales.

Generally, the cost per acquisition bidding will start a lot higher than the cost per click, but this is an all-encompassing fee that allows for impressions with no clicks and clicks with no purchase, and it boils down to what you are willing to pay for a new customer. Again the amount you bid is the *maximum* you are willing to pay for the acquisition.

Please note that to utilise this bidding option you must have already signed up to Conversion Optimiser and (at time of writing) enjoyed at least 200 conversions within the past 30 days.

Budget Optimiser (AdWords-lite) is certainly the option to choose if you're already feeling bamboozled with the array of choices and decisions you need to make in terms of setting up and running an AdWords campaign. With Budget Optimiser you decide on a monthly budget, sit back and relax ... Google will then optimise the display of all of your ads to try to get your budget spent on clicks. It works fine if your only goal is to maximise the number of clicks you receive in any given month, but it leaves you with very little control. In fairness you will spend your budget and you will get traffic. At first glance, that might seem quite attractive, but you will lose the ability to specify the times your ads are shown, which may affect your conversion rate and your preferences over the position in which your ad is displayed, which in turn will affect your cost per click.

Preferred Cost Bidding: If you are looking for a bit more control over your ad spend while still maintaining control over your ads timing, then Preferred Cost Bidding allows you to more closely dictate how much your average cost per click will be, as opposed to setting a maximum bid and then waiting for Google to tell you what your average cost per click turned out to be.

Preferred cost bidding works best once you actually have an AdWords history – i.e. if over the past few months your ads have performed better when you've been paying an average price of say £0.65, then you might want to stipulate this as your preferred bid. If, however, you are new to AdWords, then the flexibility of stipulating a maximum bid will return far more useful data in terms of best position, best time of day and more flexibility to compete with competitors who may be altering their bid prices daily or weekly.

Keeping the focus narrow

I can't stress enough how good management of your AdWords campaign will pay off in the end. This starts with how you structure/name your ads and filters down to the amount and detail of the keywords you are bidding on. One advert will simply not be sufficient to cover the aims, goals and desires for every user searching for all of those keywords – their interest is too broad and the ad will fail – either because it's too vague to entice users to click through, or too many users click through but don't then do anything on your site, thus costing you a tremendous amount of cash for no return.

It is far better to have a single ad completely tailored for one keyword, and thus have a portfolio of fifty ads running to cover your keyword range, than to pin your hopes and the success of your AdWords campaign on the back of a couple of generic 'they'll do' crowd-pleasers.

It does take time to set up numerous ads, and it does take time to monitor their performance and continue to test and tweak them to improve that performance, but it's time well spent and can be the difference between e-business success and abject failure.

Position Preference: On first appearance, this might seem to be a somewhat strange option. In everything we do, and especially when that something has anything whatsoever to do with the words *Google, ranking* or *position*, we all crave for the top spot. To be number 1 seems to be king, the alpha, a reason to live! And yet Google offer advertisers the opportunity to shun this coveted position – to actually express a preference for something lower. 'Why?' I hear you ask. Well, there is a school of thought that maintains that the top spot or even the top three spots aren't the be-all and end-all. Months of stats regarding previous and existing ad campaigns can indeed show that some ads, for some keywords, in some industries, actually do markedly better in terms of CTR, price and users' action once they've clicked through in, say, positions 4, 5 or 6, or even position 10. It's strange, but true. It could be that Google users are more switched on than many advertisers give them credit for – they know what AdWords are and even how they work, and therefore deliberately do not choose to go with the advertiser who is perceived to be bidding the most money per click. Just out of defiances, the users will actually seek out an ad lower down the list and click there instead. There is also a case for saying that some users will deliberately ignore the ads placed by Google above the natural search results – perceiving these ads to be sponsored, they are therefore unwilling to click.

Another possibility is that users do not see these ads at all because they blend into the search results, meaning that they are in fact more likely to click on the ads served on the right-hand side of the page – and if the users click on the top AdWord on the right, that is in fact ad number 3 or 4. For this reason, and because Google will only show two or three ads at the top of the search results, by deliberately opting for a preference of position 3 or 4, you might enjoy a better CTR than the ads served in position 1 or 2.

The jury's out on this, and what works for one business may or may not work for you, but what is clear is that it works enough for Google to offer you the chance to choose a position preference should you want to. Review your ads and experiment with positioning to see what works for you – all of the information is there for you to make an informed decision both before and after any change to your ad and you'll quickly know whether it's working for you or not.

Don't get carried away

Someone, somewhere will always have a bigger pot of cash than you. That's life; get over it. You might find that the particular keywords you are interested in are already hotly contested and bid prices are high. Don't despair – the number 1 AdWord position is not the only position that means success.

Although it's difficult to concede defeat, you may only be able to afford to be at position 5 or 6. Even so, it's still worth entering the race. If you get your ad right and impress Google with a commanding CTR, you will rise up the rankings without having to spend any more money – and possibly by spending less money.

When you're first deciding how much you are willing to bid on a keyword, you would be wise to see what the recommended bid value is. However, this is your campaign so it is fundamentally your choice. Make a decision based on what you can afford, and pay attention to the CTR and how those users convert into customers on your site – it could be that you actually make more money for your business with an ad placed at position 6, 7, 8, etc., than when you've broken the bank to be number 1.

Case Study – Logo Warehouse

It's more serendipity than anything else, but it so happens that at the time of writing this book I am also about to launch an online business selling pre-designed logo templates and offering a bespoke logo design service – all at very reasonable prices. The website is www.logo-warehouse.co.uk and it will be a useful exercise for you, and for me, to look at examples of what works and what doesn't through the lens of a live and current AdWords campaign.

So, a few weeks before launch, I'm ready to take a look at the current market and begin to make plans about how I'm going to tackle my AdWords campaign. Of course, I looked into the market when I was first planning the business, but that was a number of months ago and, as we all know, the entire online landscape can change (both positively and negatively) in a short time span. Hence, this exercise is always worth repeating.

The first thing I need to do is get a feel for the market. There are a number of keywords I'm going to want to bid on (more of this in chapter 3) but for now let's take a look at 'logo templates' and 'bespoke logo design', which are the phrases I used to describe the business and seem as a good a place as any to begin.

Looking at the results shown in figures 1 and 2, it's quite clear I'm not the only player in the market and I'm certainly not the only one who is interested in AdWords. Fear not, competition is healthy and to see so many other companies all trying to capture the same market gives me confidence that AdWords works for my industry – if it didn't, do you really think so many companies would continue to pay for a service with little or no return? Yes, it's going to cost me a bit more per click, but I've factored that into my pricing model. Let's get started.

Defining campaigns and ad groups

The ultimate success of your relationship with Google depends on the performance of your ad campaign, and, therefore, as you're going to be checking data relating to your campaign a lot over the

A screen capture of a Google search results page for "Logo templates":

Web Images Maps News Shopping Mail more ▼

Google — Logo templates — Search — Advanced Search / Preferences

Search: ⦿ the web ◯ pages from the UK

Web

LOGO DESIGN TEMPLATE
www.25PoundLogo.co.uk   Did You Know That You Can Have 6 **Logo** Samples For Just £25?. Try it!

In a Hurry? DIY **Logo** £29
www.logofresh.com   Only pay if you get what you want Save 6 logos online for free today

Online **Logo** Design Tool
www.Logomaker.com   Use Our Simple **Logo** Creation Tool To Build Striking Custom Logos!

Free **Logo Templates** – Free Company **Logo** – Free Website Design ...
Free **logo templates**, free company **logo**, free **logo** design and free web page layouts.
www.templatesbox.com/free-logo-templates/index.htm - 40k - Cached - Similar pages

Logo Templates – Company **Logo** - **Logo** Design – **Templates** Box
TemplatesBox.com provides **logo** design, **logo templates**, corporate **logo** and much more
webmaster resources.
www.templatesbox.com/premium-templates/logo-templates/ - 39k - Cached - Similar pages
More results from www.templatesbox.com »

Logo templates from **Template** Monster for **logo** design
The main difference between a regular **logo** and **Logo Templates** is that **Logo Templates**
are developed to reflect the main idea of the industry not the ...
www.templatemonster.com/logo-templates.php - 56k - Cached - Similar pages

Custom **Logo** Design, Professional **Logo** Design, **Logo Templates**
logolabs offers professional **logo** design, pre made **logo templates**, stationery design for your
business at affordable rates. We are to help you to raise ...
www.logolabs.com/ - 39k - Cached - Similar pages

Logo design, pre-made **logo** design and stationery
a **logo** design that can represent your business and make a positive impact. logos. Partner
Links. Website **Templates**. Large Web **Template** Collection ...
www.logomaid.com/ - 20k - Cached - Similar pages

Free Website **Templates**, Free **Logo Templates**, Free Newsletter ...

Figure 1 The keyword 'logo templates' is very popular with advertisers - ads are being displayed on the right hand side of the page and at the top. I'm guessing that competition for this keyword is fierce.

bespoke logo design - Google Sear
http://www.google.co.uk/search?hl=en&q=bespoke+logo+design&btnG=Google+
Apple .Mac Amazon eBay News (461) Nicki istock Apple (77) Amazon eBay Yahoo!
Web Images Maps News Shopping Mail more
Google
bespoke logo design
Search
Advanced Search
Preferences
Search: the web pages from the UK
Web
Bespoke logo design
www.creativeorigin.co.uk Professional logo design Fixed fee of £450, start-to-finish.
Creative logo design
www.businesslogo.net fuel your brand in 3 business days through a professional logo design
Design Your Own Logo £29
www.logofresh.com Enjoy choosing font, logo, colours Save 6 Logos Free Online in 10 mins
Bespoke LOGO DESIGN from Bristol's Clear Design UK
Professional logo design from Clear Design UK - Engaging logos that stand out from the clutter. Avoid the risks associated with open-ended hourly rates...
www.cleardesignuk.com/professional-logo-design.html - 9k - Cached - Similar pages
Startups | Bespoke Logo Design
Bespoke Logo Design. leedjc started this topic @ 19:11 on 13/08/2006 .... RE: RE: Bespoke Logo Design. #209100 in reply to #209099 ...
www.startups.co.uk/ 6678842909429769358/bespoke-logo-design.html - 84k - Cached - Similar pages
Web design and SEO specialists London, Search Engine Optimization ...
MakeITlive is a web design and development, seo company based in London. ... LOGO DESIGN. Artworks and logos add something special to your web site and you ...
makeitlive.co.uk/ - 17k - Cached - Similar pages
Bespoke Website Design - Getting a Website Designed
Search Engine Promotion : Website Design : SEO Consultancy : Logo Design : Bristol Based Designers ... Your bespoke design will attract visitors from afar. ...
www.jet-web.co.uk/bespoke-website-design.htm - 14k - Cached - Similar pages
Bespoke web site design, bespoke website design London
Empower Inc Logo ... We supply highly innovative bespoke web design and development as well as creating smart solutions for your online communications needs ...
www.empowerinc.org.uk/ - 13k - Cached - Similar pages
Bespoke logo design to suit everyone's requirements and budget ...
custom logo design is catered for here as well as re-purposing existing logos for web, print or signage. Logos can be supplied in pixel and vector format as ...

Figure 2 The keyword 'bespoke logo design' is very popular with advertisers – ads are being displayed on the right-hand side of the page and at the top. I'm guessing that competition for this keyword is fierce

coming weeks and months, it makes sense to structure your campaign in a logical way. This structure should not just be a way that makes sense to you; it must be in a form that can be explained with ease to a colleague.

Your first major decision therefore is to define a structure that is going to work for you now and that is also scalable. What's best: create a new *campaign* or a new *ad group?*

Well, the important thing to remember here is the different settings relating to these two choices. Campaigns have 'macro'-level settings – your target language/s, geographic locations, distribution preferences, start and end dates and, of course, a daily budget. You can create up to twenty-five campaigns. Ad groups have 'micro'-level settings – your list of keywords, destination URLs, maximum CPC and, of course, the ads themselves. There is a maximum level of one hundred ad groups within a single campaign.

So what dictates whether a campaign or an ad group is required? It's up to you. What I would say is that to get big, you need to think big and therefore plan for the future and look at everything at campaign level rather than ad group level. For Logo Warehouse, I have two campaigns, one for the template logo aspect of the business and one for bespoke logo design. The two sides of the business are different cost centres for me – they bring in different amounts of revenue – and therefore they have separate and very different daily budgets. With my Toytopia business, each 'product type' had its own campaign. For instance, we had a distinct campaign for clothing and within that campaign were several ad groups, such as t-shirts, shoes, bibs, etc. Similarly, with the toys, 'push-along toys' had its own campaign, as did 'plush toys'.

Separate campaigns should certainly be employed if there is a different head of department for each section of your business and there is no doubt that you should use multiple campaigns if multiple users have access to your company's Google account – the last thing you want is for your campaign performance to suffer because of a colleague's failings!

Setting up more campaigns than you need is not a tremendous problem – after all it's just an extra click of the mouse to drop down to ad group level – but not setting up enough campaigns can prove awkward in the future. Managing your campaigns and ad groups is straightforward if you make it manageable from the start. You will probably need to make alterations as time progresses so it is important to think through how things might evolve.

Logo Warehouse - the basic campaign

To get me started as quickly as possible, I want to have a campaign that is easy to measure in terms of effectiveness and not too demanding on my bank account. A common mistake is to want to serve your ad around the world, but if you sell garden gnomes and your website is priced in pounds sterling, it's unlikely that you're going to have many customers in Asia or South America. Also, if your website is written in English, there's little point paying for an advert that will display to Japanese users …

There are, of course, exceptions to the rule, and you'll know who and where your market is. But, for now, start small and grow into territories rather than trying to use a scattergun approach and hoping that something will stick. If you can't do a good job in your own back yard, you're going to be hard pushed to break into the rest of world. Once you've proven that your AdWords campaign works in the UK market, feel free to spread your wings further afield ... but not until then!

I'll start with just three adverts, all with slightly different messages. My target countries are the UK and Ireland and, so as not to alienate readers, I will be using a modest budget of £5.00 per day (or about £150 per month) to get my AdWords campaign underway. I'm still a few weeks away from launch, but I want my ads to be ready to go. The moment my site goes live, I'll give Google my payment details and the ads will be served (see figures 3, 4, 5 and 6) ...

The differences between the ads are very slight but it's these subtleties of language and change of focus that can make or break an AdWords campaign. In my research into the logo design market, it became evident that price was a major factor. So, to compete effectively it's clear I must be up-front about my pricing, which I have done in my example ads.

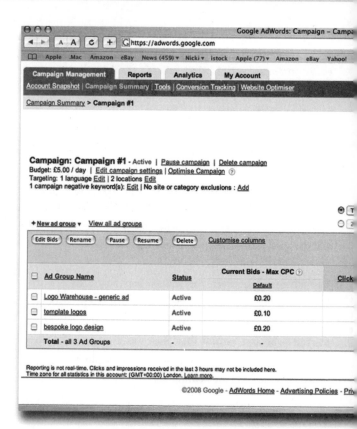

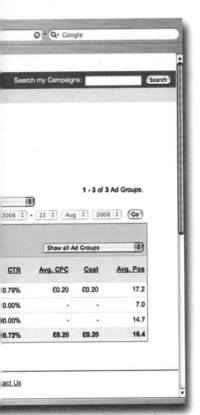

Figure 3 My basic campaign has just three adverts (figures 4, 5 and 6), they will only be displayed in the UK and Ireland and my entire budget is capped at £5.00 per day

Logo Design & Branding
Template Logos and Bespoke Design
Instant affordable brand identity
www.logo-warehouse.co.uk

Figure 4 Advert 1: this is my generic advert focusing on both template logos and bespoke design

Professional Logo Designs
Template Logos from £29
Instant affordable brand identity
www.logo-warehouse.co.uk

Figure 5 Advert 2: this is my 'template' advert, which only mentions template designs

Bespoke Logo Designs
Receive 8 unique designs
Unlimited revisions £199
www.logo-warehouse.co.uk

Figure 6 Advert 3: this is my 'bespoke' advert, which focuses on the bespoke aspect of the business

With any new campaign and first venture into Google AdWords, I want to stress that you should start small and build up your campaign rather than trying to be all things to all people and spending a small fortune on an ineffective – or, worse, inconclusive – campaign. Data from your early weeks will quickly confirm what keywords are working for you, and more importantly what *negative* keywords you need to employ to improve your CTR (see page 69 for more on this). Start off too big, with an unmanageable list of keywords, and you'll become swamped and confused; inevitably the campaign will be both expensive and a failure.

Reinventing the wheel?

Testing and rewriting is critical to a successful AdWords campaign – keep an eye on not just your own ads, but the ads and the activity of your competitors. While this book (or in fact any book) cannot tell you how to write the perfect ad for your business, in a strange way, your competitors can. Start with the basics – type in one of the keywords you are bidding on already, or intend to bid on, and pay attention to the results. This test can be repeated as often as you like: I would try for every two hours, to allow for any competitor settings to show themselves, such as accelerated delivery, or a limited daily spend coming into effect. What you will notice is either the same ad (or a range of ads from the same business) coming up top, or you'll notice a real eclectic mix of ads all changing position with each search. Over a number of days, and especially over the coming weeks, a pattern will emerge. If there is a consistent ad or a selection of consistent ads always in the top spots then it's pretty safe to assume that these ads are working for the advertiser. Learn from them, emulate, and ultimately improve on them.

It's not cheating. It's not taking the easy option – it's competitor analysis. What phrases are they using? What aspects of their ad can you incorporate into yours? What your competitors are doing should form the basis of your own campaign. This becomes your opening gambit and then the real testing begins as you begin to incorporate small alterations that will hopefully become improvements resulting in a greater CTR and, hopefully, a lower bid price.

Be sure to empty your cache and/or temporary Internet files before any test. Otherwise, you run the risk of seeing a cached version of the Google search results page.

Ad position

Every industry is different and every keyword is different, but chances are there are at least a few competitors running AdWord campaigns for the same keywords as you. A bit of competition is healthy, and should even be encouraged. However, where it gets messy is if there are more than ten advertisers because there are only ten positions for AdWord ads on any search results page. Therefore, if you're ad is positioned at number 11 or beyond, it's not being displayed on the first page of those results and I'm afraid that's not of much value to you. It's certainly true that some users will click through to page 2 and beyond to find what they are looking for, but their focus at this stage will very much be on the organic or natural listings and they will probably be searching for something very specific – so you're ad's not going to work effectively.

Now it could be that you're happy with the cheap bid price and the very occasional click-through – but, don't forget, if the CTR drops too low or never picks up, then Google is going to disable the ad, so it's of little use being in that position. Personally, if I can't afford to be in the top 10 ad positions, then I kill the ad and look at investing the cash in more niche keywords in which I can compete.

Number 1 isn't everything

Remember: as hard as it might be to believe, the number 1 spot isn't always the best. Later on in the book we'll see how being number 3 or 4 can actually produce a far higher ROI for your business, but for now I just want to warn against getting sucked into a bidding war with another advertiser because you both want to be number 1. It happens easily – either you come along and decide to oust the current incumbent by bidding higher, and they respond ... or you are enjoying the top spot and a young pretender comes along and outbids you ... before long, you both increase your bids, which results in counter-bid after counter-bid. Now that war's broken out, the two advertisers fighting for the top spot are paying an average price per click of £3 or £4 plus, yet the bidding for position 3 remains at a modest £0.45. The advertiser is still getting click-throughs at position 3 and we can guess those click-throughs are converting to customers on the site. So, while you two monkeys are having a private spat over the number 1 spot, the price per new customer is far higher than you should be paying.

Only Google wins when there's a bidding war. Set yourself a limit – a percentage amount you are willing to rise up to from your initial bid – and stick to it. Once there's somebody out there who's willing to keep on upping the ante, back away. Positions 3, 4 and 7 are just as viable and can be just as profitable.

A word of warning

Click fraud happens. Now, the good news is that Google has tools in place to detect an obvious attempt by a single IP address (read: a nefarious individual, probably a competitor) to click on your ad multiple times, which would ordinarily cost you a lot of money. Where click fraud is detected you will be refunded, but it's still in your interest to monitor your log files for IP addresses on click-throughs and to notice any suspicious activity. Low-level fraud will get through, undetected, and it will be costing you money, but I'm afraid there's not a tremendous amount you can do about it. No doubt when you were researching your keywords you clicked on some ads to see what lay at the destination URL, and in turn competitors will do the same to you. During the process of writing this book I have clicked on thousands of ads with absolutely no intention of buying anything from the advertisers.

It's frustrating, it's expensive (very, if you happen to be in an industry where clicks for your keywords are many pounds each) and it will negatively affect your CTR. But, please, don't be tempted to exacerbate the problem by becoming trigger-happy yourself. It's not big, it's not clever, and it doesn't impress the girls. Let's face it, it wouldn't take much for Google to marry up the IP address of your AdWords account with a problem IP address for one of your competitors ... at best, your campaign will be shut down instantaneously and your website removed from the Google index; at worst, you could be on the receiving end of a lawsuit.

mputer, businesswoman, bus

document, efficiency, electro

ok, people, person, plan, pla

woman, work, young commu

web, corporate, debate, dialo

npany, job, business, pe

pretty, sensual, service, corpo

woman, work, young, commu

, dialogue, document, efficie

top, matching, notebook, pe

art, smile, sophisticated, str

corporate debate dia

3

The importance of keywords

In praise of the long tail

I love the long tail. It is focusing on the long tail of products that has allowed companies like The Book Depository and Play.com to enter the busy and competitive book/DVD/games retail market and become serious players in only a few years, despite the perceived belief that Amazon had online sales all sewn up.

In terms of AdWords and choosing your keywords, the long tail is of paramount importance, especially if you are looking to find a niche for yourself or budget constraints mean that you can't possibly compete with the big boys in terms of the critical (read: generic) keywords in your particular industry.

Google offers a keyword search as part of the 'AdWords Dashboard', but it's worth bidding on words you've thought of yourself – it's your industry, after all, and that knowledge you have of the market is just as important as Google's view of the related words. It's also worth looking elsewhere for keyword suggestions, such as www.nichebot.com and www.wordtracker.com. Both of these sites recently started charging for their services, but if you're taking your AdWords campaign seriously it's a necessary expense.

There are top-level keywords in every single industry. As an online toy-seller I was obsessed with the keyword 'toys', but it quickly became apparent that I was up against *ToysRUs* and *ToyMaster*, even though we were in different markets. On long-term marketing spend, I simply couldn't compete. The click-throughs we did get when we paid over the odds for the keyword 'toys' weren't converting to sales. What was the matter? The answer was that we had a specialist offering – traditional-style wooden toys, finger puppets, pram toys and off-the-wall clothing and footwear. The simple fact is, people who type in the word 'toys' were looking for the latest craze, invariably made out of plastic, which had enjoyed advertising on the television. That wasn't the sort of stuff we sold. OK, we sold toys, but not the *toys* that these people were looking for.

The answer: go niche. Be specific. Explore the long tail. I optimised our ads to be specific, not generic – *wooden toys, push-along toys* etc., and the results were staggering. Suddenly we were enjoying a higher CTR and, more importantly, a higher conversion ratio. In simple terms we were attracting the right sort of customers, who *were* interested in buying from our offering, and more of them were committing to purchase.

Once you have decided on your long-tail keywords, don't forget to divide them into sensible and focused ad groups. Only then can you track how effective they are.

Ad group convention

We all get a bit carried away when first setting up an AdWords campaign – we want our ad to be visible in every country and we want it to be displayed whenever a huge list of keywords is queried by a user. Stop! Think!

AdWords works best when a targeted ad is precision tailored for one or a small selection of keywords. One generic ad serving fifty keywords won't be all things to all people; it will just be ignored (and quite quickly disabled by Google). Or, worse, it will attract a high CTR but with users then realising they don't want anything to do with you or your website – after they have already cost you money.

It's far better to break down your selection of keywords into small, themed and easy-to-manage groups. It doesn't matter how many groups you create – you can have up to 100 ads per ad group – just make the task manageable and logical and this will result in your ads for those groups being far more effective.

Internet users are cash rich, time poor and can't spell

We are all guilty of using Google Search without a care in the world for spelling, grammar or punctuation. How many times have you typed something like 'cassic cars' and Google has helpfully asked 'Did you mean classic cars?' We all do it, and that's something you should remember when you're looking to expand your keywords and the size of your campaign. My first book, *The Bloke's Guide To Pregnancy*, sells very well through my ads, but sales almost doubled once I began to run three additional ads for *Blokes Guide*, *Blokesguide* and *Blokes' Guide*. The best bit is that bidding on misspelled and merged keywords can get you a surprising amount of traffic and a good CTR at a fraction of the cost!

Negative keywords

I know it's natural to want to cast your net as wide as possible and to strive to warmly welcome all newcomers. And, yes, it's correct that we don't truly know what a user's actions are going to be until they hit your site. But I can tell you that after a few weeks, when you start seeing the pounds going out for click-throughs that aren't converting, you tend to lose whatever egalitarian views you might have had and come over all fascist.

Negative keywords give you some freedom to limit the kind of searches, and therefore the kind of user, you might otherwise attract.

Negative keywords allow you to specify when you don't want your ad to be shown. In the example of Logo Warehouse, I charge for the logos on offer, so I want bargain hunters to refrain from clicking on my ads. I've therefore listed 'free' as a negative keyword because I'm a business; I'm not a charity.

In the case of my toy business, as well as having a long list of keywords I did want to bid on – *push-along toys, wooden building blocks, puppets*, etc. – it was very easy to keep the wrong sort of customer away by determining what they might accidentally think I might sell – *Transformers, Pokemon, SexToys*, etc. The negative keyword list was very long indeed.

If the glut of phone calls we received from customers asking for these latter products was any indication of demand, then we must have saved thousands and thousands of pounds in what would have been wasted click-throughs on our AdWords. And if you're wondering why we didn't decide to sell these products if demand was so high, the truth is we considered it, but the market is very faddish and the mark up on those products is rubbish.

Your negative keyword list will constantly grow because you won't think of everything at first. It is only as the clicks begin to come through and you are able to analyse the actual phrases being used that you'll notice a pattern of searchers who enter certain words, along with the keyword you're targeting, but are not converting once they've clicked through. These searches are costing you money and you need to add the problem keywords to your negative list. If you sell products or services at a regular or premium rate, then deter the bargain hunters from the outset by including negative keywords such as 'discount', 'free', 'cheap' and 'bargain'. If you only sell ceramic garden gnomes, then add 'plastic' and 'wooden' as negative keywords.

The more specific you can be with your description in your ad, the more likely it is that you'll get the right sort of user clicking through and hopefully becoming a customer. If you're selling plasma TVs, then run specific ads for each of the brand names you

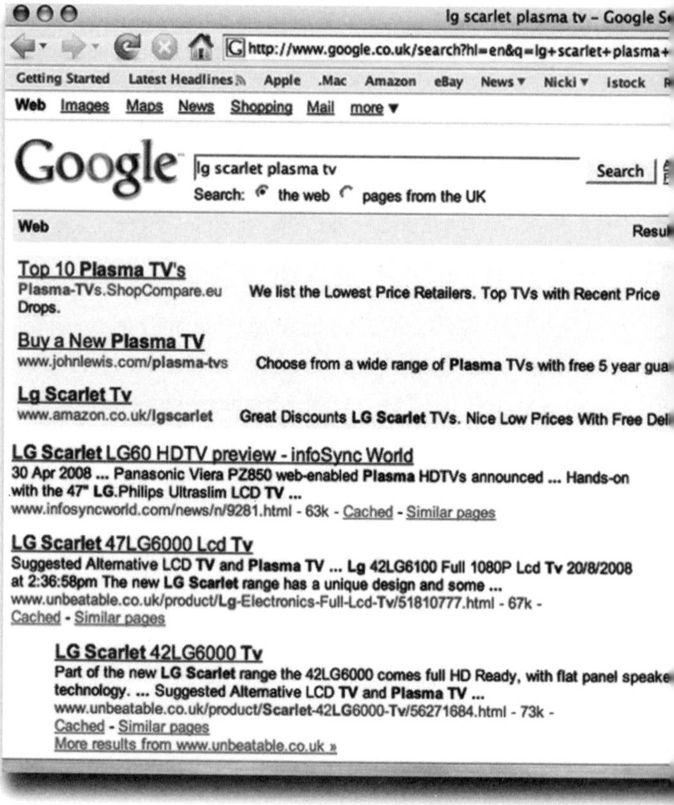
lg scarlet plasma tv – Google S
http://www.google.co.uk/search?hl=en&q=lg+scarlet+plasma+
Getting Started
Latest Headlines
Apple
.Mac
Amazon
eBay
News
Nicki
istock
Web
Images
Maps
News
Shopping
Mail
more
Google
lg scarlet plasma tv
Search
Search: the web pages from the UK
Web
Top 10 Plasma TV's
Plasma-TVs.ShopCompare.eu
We list the Lowest Price Retailers. Top TVs with Recent Price Drops.
Buy a New Plasma TV
www.johnlewis.com/plasma-tvs
Choose from a wide range of Plasma TVs with free 5 year gua
Lg Scarlet Tv
www.amazon.co.uk/lgscarlet
Great Discounts LG Scarlet TVs. Nice Low Prices With Free Del
LG Scarlet LG60 HDTV preview - infoSync World
30 Apr 2008 ... Panasonic Viera PZ850 web-enabled Plasma HDTVs announced ... Hands-on with the 47" LG.Philips Ultraslim LCD TV ...
www.infosyncworld.com/news/n/9281.html - 63k - Cached - Similar pages
LG Scarlet 47LG6000 Lcd Tv
Suggested Alternative LCD TV and Plasma TV ... Lg 42LG6100 Full 1080P Lcd Tv 20/8/2008 at 2:36:58pm The new LG Scarlet range has a unique design and some ...
www.unbeatable.co.uk/product/Lg-Electronics-Full-Lcd-Tv/51810777.html - 67k - Cached - Similar pages
LG Scarlet 42LG6000 Tv
Part of the new LG Scarlet range the 42LG6000 comes full HD Ready, with flat panel speake technology. ... Suggested Alternative LCD TV and Plasma TV ...
www.unbeatable.co.uk/product/Scarlet-42LG6000-Tv/56271684.html - 73k - Cached - Similar pages
More results from www.unbeatable.co.uk »

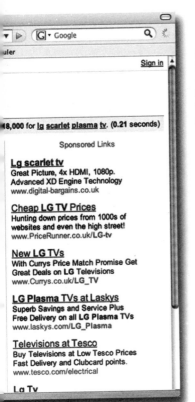

Figure 7 The ad I will click on will be the ad that best represents my search – in this case, those ads that acknowledge not just LG the manufacturer, but the specific Scarlet range

carry – and, on top of that, include the model or series type. For example, I recently saw an advert on the TV for the Scarlet Plasma TV from LG. I want more information and I turn to Google. Figure 7 shows what I found.

So, I have a few choices. There are a couple of links in the organic listings that mention both LG the manufacturer and the Scarlet range of TVs and there are two ads which do the same. My natural instinct on this occasion was to click the ad placed at the top of the right hand side – the ad in position 4. Not only has the use of dynamic keywords for the headline confirmed that this ad will answer my need, the brand and the range are also reinforced within the ad content. I'm a click-through and if I had received a more generous advance for writing this book from my publisher, I would have been a customer! For now, I'll have to stick with my fourteen-inch black and white TV.

succentoi

succinere

success

nation

positior

achieve

4

Getting started with AdWords

What determines whether your ad appears at the top of the page or on the right?

Nothing ... well, nothing you can alter or influence. It's Google's thing: sometimes all the ads are placed on the right of the page and sometimes there are two at the top of the page. They're not separate or more expensive positions; they're AdWords ads. It's just they tend to be displayed when a particular keyword is popular and therefore there's a lot of advertiser demand. Look at it as a reward scheme – those keywords that are real money-spinners for Google are worth encouraging. Those companies that are prepared to bid the most are making the most money per click for Google, and therefore it makes complete sense for Google to give them the top spot – quite literally at the top of the page. If the keywords you're bidding on are either in low demand or relatively cheap, your ad will be displayed on the right of the page.

Toeing the '###!!!!L@@K & FEEL!!!!###' line

Going back to chapter 1 briefly, you'll remember that part of Google's success and why users come back again and again is its refreshingly simple and clean look. Compared with the noisy Yahoo! and Alta Vista homepages, Google's clean white space makes searching almost a pleasure and users flock to use its service, which made Google the number 1 search engine very quickly. Google's homepage is possibly the most valuable real estate on the World Wide Web. I have no doubt that lots and lots of companies have offered eye-watering amounts of cash to be advertised there and they've all been refused. Google doesn't like noise. Google doesn't like garish. Google doesn't like blatant commercialism. Google's business model and huge success has proven categorically that simplicity works effectively and that's why Google ain't going to tolerate any shenanigans from you!

Familiarise yourself with Google's AdWords Programme Service Agreement – it is strictly enforced. In a nutshell, the look and feel of your ads should err on the side of caution. Any ads that make excessive use of CAPS and !!!!!!! will be removed – in fact, the rule is you're only allowed to use one exclamation mark! Don't be tempted to try it to see how long your advert will last (I've done that for you and about three weeks is the best I've managed). It's a waste of your time when you could be utilising and benefiting from a 'proper' ad that's bringing prospects to your site. Google does have the power and right to cancel your AdWords account completely, especially if you are a habitual offender – and let's face it, they have the technology to easily check your organic listings and tactics too. It doesn't take a genius to realise that if you're pushing it in terms of your AdWords campaign, it might attract a closer investigation of your overall relationship with Google. The net result could be a total removal from the Google index, and you really don't want that! Play it safe, play it cool and craft your ads well.

Keep the message going

For AdWords to be most effective in terms of sales for you, there must be a relevant relationship between the sales message you display in your ad and the content of the page the user finds at the destination URL. It's not good enough to mention sexy bras in your ad and then point users to your generic lingerie homepage. Point the user to a specific page on your site that reinforces the ad. In the case above, bring them to your bra page, or to a specific bra product detail page that is selling for the price you quoted in the ad.

Don't expect users to arrive at your homepage and willingly navigate through your site to find the offer, the deal or the free gift you promised in your ad. If what they want isn't there to greet them on their arrival at the destination URL, then they are going to abandon your site and, although you'll get the credit in your CTR, you won't have made any money – only lost it.

The importance of quality

Google's aim is to serve the best search results to its users. Along with those search results come AdWords, and Google is obsessed with ensuring that the ads are relevant and beneficial to the users, so as not to damage the hard work that's been done in building Google Search. That's why your ads are scored on relevancy and receive a quality score; that's why there are strict editorial rules; and that's why frequent offenders have their accounts suspended!

The good news is that if you are playing by the rules and your ads are targeted and effective, you will be rewarded, and this is one way your actions can speak louder than your competitor's fat wallet.

Personally, I always start my bidding high, based on what, if anything, competitors are doing around my keywords of choice. This makes the early click-throughs expensive, but it serves a number of purposes. Firstly, it lets users and competitors know that my business, or my client's business, has arrived. Secondly, this might cause a panic, and over the next few days there will be a bidding war or frenzy with competitors altering their bidding tactics and even the content of their ads. (At this point, I don't react, I just let it happen and see where I stand once the dust has settled.) Thirdly, because I've gone in high, it's likely that my generosity to Google's war-chest will be rewarded by a high rank (position 1 or 2) and users are clicking through. Now, assuming that I've got my sales message right and the content on the destination URL is to the users' liking, then I am building my reputation with Google in the form of a high CTR percentage and a good quality score and, most importantly, converting users into consumers, so the extra business is paying for the inflated ad prices.

Give it a week, and then drop your bid price – you might be surprised. As often as not, you can come in with say a 10% lower bid per click and still maintain your position! Quality score, relevancy and testing really pay off. If you've held your position for a week and you're still getting a favourable CTR, then try it again. Drop your bid by another 10%. It can go on like this – and you continue to save money while maintaining your position and the ad's effectiveness – or you can suddenly drop to position 50. As soon as that happens, increase your bid price again and you'll be back up the list. But think of all the money you've saved over the weeks (across all of your ad groups) by shaving off 10% here and there.

It might work for your keywords; it might not. Try it and find out.

SURF
TECHIE
WWW
ERROR
E-MAIL
MENU
FAST
@
ONLINE

5

Ad groups and advanced AdWords

Google Editor – more control

It's free and it works. If you want to be in truly in control of your AdWords campaign then the first thing that you are going to need, if you haven't downloaded it already, is AdWords Editor – Google's Campaign Management Application:

www.google.com/intl/en/adwordseditor/

The main advantages of using the Editor over making the alterations manually through your Google AdWords account is the ability to make mass changes and alterations over a selection of ad groups and individual ads. It also makes managing large AdWord accounts more straightforward – especially if you are working with a long list of keywords.

Your schedule

It's all in the planning. Good campaign management requires constant tinkering, rewriting, monitoring of data and reacting and interacting with Google, your competitors and your ads. But it's not going to work if you don't have a plan!

It's best to think of your AdWords campaign in terms of cycles – these can be cycles that your business already employs, such as weekly, monthly, quarterly or seasonally, but decide now how you are going to operate and stick to it.

With any campaign I am running I create a number of review dates. These are cycles, determined by a mix of calendar constraints and AdWords experience. They may or may not work for you, but it might be a good place to start as you become more and more familiar with AdWords.

Before any testing, and during testing, be sure to empty your cache.

Weekly

- *Positioning analysis* – On each of your keywords, what is your average position?

- *Position doctoring* – Any ad that is lower than the week before needs improving: alter the ad text or alter your bid. With any ads that have remained static or have improved their average position, then it is up to you whether you want to alter them. (Personally, I employ split, or A/B, testing in these circumstances and see if I can improve again on the ads' performance. More on this in chapter 7.)

Monthly

- *Re-run a keyword search* – Find out what users are looking for and ensure your AdWords ads are tailored to these keywords.

- *Add to negative keywords* – With a month of data, you'll be able to see if there are some keywords still slipping through with no conversion – add these problem keywords to your negative list.

Quarterly

With three months' data, you can really see what's working and what's not. Even if your ads or ad groups are performing well enough to have not been disabled, they may not be working for you and giving you a strong ROI. Make a decision: you can continue with alterations and testing, or you can kill the group and reassign the budget to another group or campaign.

Document everything!

It may seem like a waste of time, and a lot of the information is of course visible within your AdWords account, but I'm a big fan of cut and paste – all of the information I need is transferred into an Excel spreadsheet, tailored how I like it. The date of the next review is fixed and I stick to it.

You can go easy on yourself and start each new cycle on Monday, or the first of the month, or follow the seasons for your quarterly tasks – but personally I like to mix it up a bit. Most people will make their alterations on a Friday or more likely a Monday. (I prefer to make my weekly changes on a Wednesday so that I can react both to my own ads' performance and any alterations my competitors may have made.)

The same goes for monthly checks – I pick a random day of the month (usually the 19th) and avoid the first or last week of any month, when most of my competitors are making their own alterations.

Your ads' schedule

There's a host of reasons why interest in your ad is determined by the day of the week – you may be aware of them, or you may not. What's important is to look out for this information. Likewise, you may wish to only show your ads over the weekend, or only during the week. It may defy logic, but if over a number of weeks your conversion ratio drops significantly on a Tuesday and a Thursday, it's fine to turn off your ads for those days. Your CTR will only be calculated on the days when the ad is showing and thus, if you've got a good CTR, your bid price is going to reduce. Hence, you may be getting more customers, more cheaply by only advertising two days a week than for a full week. The beauty of having separate ad groups, or even campaigns, is that you can have different ads running for different days of the week if you so wish.

Playing with the big boys

There are times when, try as you might, you've exhausted every keyword, no matter how specialist or niche, and it's still an expensive market to be entering. Does this mean you should pack your bags and think of starting again in a completely different industry? Absolutely not! It might mean you need to rethink your pricing model to incorporate the higher cost per new customer, and it might mean that you need to revise your forecasts based on customer acquisition via Google AdWords, but, as the lottery people say, you've got to be in it to win it. So, keep going. The key is to spend even more time and effort testing and tracking your campaigns – every penny really will count and those pennies and pounds really need to be working for you in terms of conversions. Fear not: all the tools and information you need are there for you to utilise – next, we'll see how.

When things are working, bid higher!

At first, this might seem a bit odd, given that your main focus is creating ads that work well and then trying to find ways to shave a bit off the cost while still keeping a good CTR and conversion rate. However, there's a lot to be said for increasing your bid on ads that have been working well for you. At a basic level, this might throw the competition and price them out of the market. Also, if Google notices that this ad is performing well, it's going to favour your ad over others.

It could be that you increase your bid on an ad that was performing well at position 6 and suddenly it finds itself bumped up to position 1 or 2. And that might happen because you raised your bid by as little as 5p! Had you competed through the regular bid channel, you might have had to pay many times that to achieve a higher spot.

Deter unwanted click-throughs

This might also seem rather odd, but as much you want users to click through to your site, you don't want them if they're not the right sort of users. By including a deterrent within your ad – such as a price or another barrier to entry – you are encouraging those who can afford your product/service and deterring those who can't.

Click-throughs are only of value to you if those users then do something on your site – be it register, contact you or purchase. Everyone else is no more than a casual visitor, and too many of them will cost you money with no ROI.

For example, Espressio's flagship product is their extra-large hardback photo book priced at £17.99. For some users, that's too high – and therefore Espressio doesn't want their clicks – so quoting the price in the ad both attracts the users they do want and deters the users they don't.

Coffee Table Photo Book
Impressive 30cm x 30cm
Delivered to your door £17.99
www.espressio.co.uk/xlarge

Improving click-through rate

Using delimiters has improved my CTR on campaigns considerably over the years. The technique is completely *white hat SEO* (legitimate) and simply involves using a simple pair of punctuation marks as *delimiters* – quotes " " and brackets [ ] – to narrow your focus and ensure your advert is served to the niche you want.

Let's say, for example, you're bidding on 'wooden toys' – an old favourite of mine from the days when I ran Toytopia, which specialised in wooden toys, among other things.

You should bid on it in not one way, but three:

wooden toys

"wooden toys"

[wooden toys]

So, you are bidding on the term *wooden toys*, as a broad term, which means that your ad will appear any time those two words are typed in as part of a search, in any order. You are also bidding on "wooden toys", which means any search entry that includes those two words, but only in that order. And you are bidding on [wooden toys], which means searches placed on only those two words in that exact order.

Once you've added these delimiters to your search terms, you'll get a much clearer idea of what kinds of specific searches people are doing on the keywords that you're bidding on.

This technique is effective because when you bid on a 'broad' search term, you are competing against ads that are targeting all sorts of unrelated terms. You see, wooden toys is competing with all ads targeting the keyword 'toys' or 'wooden'. Broad searches can be dangerous in that they can become very expensive and can inadvertently mean you are forced to compete against competitors on the more costly terms on all manner of queries unless you have a huge list of negative keywords. Using bounded or delimited searches narrows the field and reduces the overall competition for ad space, so your cost to maintain the same average position should drop as compared to an unbounded term.

Using dynamic keywords

Dynamic keyword insertion can work wonders for your campaign. It works so well because it convinces users that your ad was tailored specifically for their search. Whatever phrase they entered into Google Search is dynamically added to your ad's headline. If they type 'Orange Garden Gnome', then the top line of your ad will read 'Orange Garden

Gnome'. Seeing the actual keywords they searched on displayed in the ad title can convince users that your business is exactly what they are looking for.

In the case of Book Depository, on any search relating to 'Books' they run the following:

[Keyword]
Free Worldwide Shipping
Big Discounts on Millions of Books
www.bookdepository.co.uk

In the case of Espressio, on any search relating to 'Photo' they run the following

[Keyword]
Create Your Photo Book
Prices from £4.99 Free P&P
www.espressio.co.uk

I use dynamic keywords, but only if my competitors are not. The situation can arise in which you have three or more advertisers all bidding on the same keyword and all employing dynamic keywords. The net effect for the user is a homogenisation of ads – they all look the same. Ironically, it is then the ad that has the fixed text (which slightly differs from the user's choice of keywords) that becomes the ad that stands out! Have a play with dynamic keywords, but watch what your competition is doing. Remember: it's good to be different.

There are lots of ways to utilise *dynamic keyword insertion* – here's a selection of examples[2]:

- ■ If you want the dynamic text to be all lower case, use {**k**eyword:Default_text}.
- ■ If you want the dynamic text to start with the first letter of the first word capitalized, use {**K**eyword:Default_text}.
- ■ If you want the dynamic text to have the first letter in caps for each word, use {**K**ey**W**ord:Default_text}.
- ■ If you want the dynamic text to have the first word to all be in caps, use {**KEY**word:Default_text}.

2. Source: http://searchengineland.com/070619-092701.php

- If you want the dynamic text to have the first word to all be in caps and the other words to start with the first letter in caps, use {**KEYW**ord:Default_text}.
- If you want the dynamic text to all be in caps, use {**KEYWORD**:Default_text}

Personally, I only use {KeyWord:Default_text} to keep the ad 'clean' looking and consistent with my static headline ads.

Remember to include alternative text

Because of the character limitations of your headline (25 characters) it sometimes happens that the search term entered by the user exceeds this maximum. If this happens your ad will display without a headline (defeating the purpose) or the headline will truncate, which looks silly. Google allows you to volunteer alternative text, which will become the default text.

In the case of the dynamic Book Depository advert above, on any search relating to 'Books' we run the following *alt text*:

[Keyword: The Book Depository]
Free Worldwide Shipping
Big Discounts on Millions of Books
www.bookdepository.co.uk

Targeting regional traffic

Depending on the nature of your business, you'll possibly want to pay most attention to attracting local business. Yes, the World Wide Web by nature is global, but if you're a vet, you're probably going to want to attract customers based within about 20 miles of your surgery in Leeds, not have anxious dog owners from Nebraska clicking through and costing you money. Within the *Target customers by location* feature, you'll notice there's a *Custom* tab. It is from here you can drop down to city level in terms of defining the audience you wish to attract by their geographical location. You can specify by postcode or city name. (I tend to set the distance parameter to 25 miles if I have a city-specific ad campaign.)

Don't forget, by using regional targeting it can open up new avenues for your business. If you sell large pieces of art or hefty wooden furniture, ordinarily you'll have had to use couriers or even freight forwarding to get your products to your customers, wherever they are.

This expensive means of getting the goods to the customer may have been incorporated into your pricing, or it means there's a substantial P&P charge added on to customer orders, but what if you could offer local customers a better deal? For anyone ordering within 25 miles, you might even be able to deliver it yourself? How does that alter your costs, and what does it mean for the customer? Regional targeting opens up lots of new opportunities and, ironically, the World Wide Web can introduce you to a whole host of local people interested in your products – they just weren't aware that you were around the corner!

As a slight aside, personally, I don't think Google has quite figured out how to assure users' geographic location as accurately as they maintain, and therefore it is advised you run a local campaign and a generic campaign. Using the vet example above, I would run a city-targeted campaign for 'Vet, Leeds' and a generic ad with the keywords 'Vet, Leeds'. Yes, it's a bit more costly, but a few weeks of data will show you which one is performing for you, if not both, and you can adapt from there.

Time please, gentlemen

Even if your campaign is limited to a UK audience and only showing through Google Search, time can and will play a role in who clicks through on your ad and what they then do on your site. This will of course depend on your industry, but look out for trends and patterns of when you're receiving your best CTR and your best conversion rate. *Automatic bid adjustment* can be your best friend here – increasing your bid during your 'peak hours', and therefore your ad's position, can be hugely beneficial. Is there a spike during lunch hours? What about first thing in the morning, or towards the late afternoon when workers' minds are no longer on the task they're being paid for? The information is there, so use it.

Surfing under the influence...

This is only conjecture, but I have seen enough evidence to suggest that there are certainly sales to be made after pubs kick out. Give it a month to prove or disprove my theory but for a number of businesses (including wooden toys!) I've increased my bids during the hours of 22.00 and 01.00, attained a temporary higher position and reaped the rewards of dads (and mums) coming home from a night on the town and splashing out a small fortune on a gift for little Freddie. The increased bid might only be 10-20%, which may equate to pennies, but the drunk pound is generous and covers the increased cost quite nicely. One for yourself, mate!

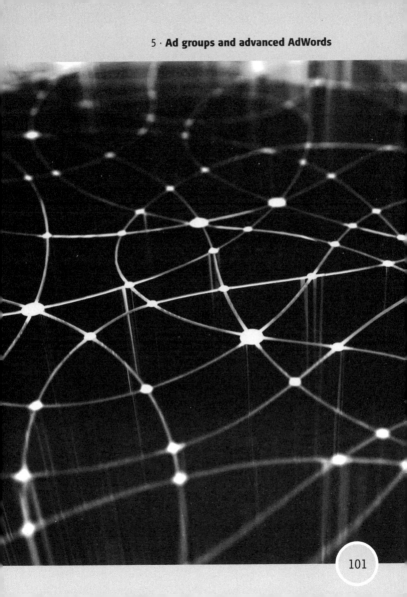

6

Writing killer ads

Sell, sell, sell

We all have our own ways of writing sales messages. Certainly within the constraints of the tight character count on AdWords, good ad writing really is a fine art. Different messages and styles work for different industries and only by testing your ads will you know what works for your business.

As an experiment do try the 'three mentions' rule – that is, whatever your core keyword for this particular ad group, be sure to mention it three times in your ad. This can be in the header and twice in the text, or even include a mention in the display URL. However you do it, try it and see what happens. It could be too much of a 'hard sell' for your business, but equally it could be the most successful ad you ever run.

Squeeze every single character

Using the display URL to continue your sales message is a good tactic. There's a lot to be said for including 'power' words within the URL that add to the overall message of the ad:

www.bookdespository.co.uk/freebook
www.bookdepository.co.uk/buy1get1free

If this is the angle you'd like to pursue, then by all means go for it and don't forget that if you require up to four more characters you can always remove the 'www.' from the start of the display URL.

Squeezing everything in
it's hard work sometimes making
sure can say everthing you want
shavingoffthewww.com/makesmoreroom

Don't forget that the display URL is not actually determining the destination address. Therefore the rules of capitalisation can extend to the display URL. Which of the following is going to grab your attention?

www.bookdepository.co.uk/freebook

or

www.BookDepository.co.uk/FreeBook

Less is more

Contrary to our natural marketing instinct about maxing out the sales message within the limited word count available, I can't stress enough how important it is to continually play with your ad copy and explore all possibilities – to see what works for your business. Towards the end of my AdWords campaign with Toytopia, there were more and more advertisers bidding on 'my' keywords, and the search pages were beginning to get very busy with hard-sell ads all vying for attention.

I'll admit that I didn't have much faith in the softly, softly approach being successful, but you have to give these things a try ... and I was pleasantly surprised. In between all of that noise on the page, users chose the most simple of ads on offer. I deliberately chose to be in position 5 and the clicks came flooding through. This turned out to be one of my most successful ads for the keyword 'Wooden Toys':

```
Wooden Toys _____

looking for a good home...
www.toytopia.co.uk
```

Try something similar; it might just work!

They know ...

While remembering to include a call to action within your ad – be it an attractive price point or an invitation to register – don't be tempted to include 'click here'. For a start, Google will not approve and the ad will be removed, but, more importantly it is a waste of words and a bit of an insult to your potential customers – they know to click it if they're interested; they managed to boot up their computers, launch a web browser, and enter a keyword into Google Search to find your ad. Users know what to do next. Here are some calls to action that are allowed, if you're stuck:

- Download Our Catalogue
- Browse Our Range
- Free Report
- Free Quotation

- Apply Now
- Sign Up Now
- Free Demo
- Free Trial

It may just be down to personal taste, but I am not a huge fan of using the word 'Buy' within AdWords. I think it's pretty clear that all AdWords adverts are promoting a service or a product that customers will need to purchase, so adding the word 'Buy' is somewhat superfluous and a waste of your very limited word count. Use your word count to promote the product or service by name and word it in such a way that users will want to click through and buy without you spelling it out.

Words that can be effective within your ad (depending on your business) are those relating to time – we're all busy, and your potential customers are no different. 'Sign up now', 'Act now', 'Act today' and 'Limited offer' have all been used extremely well on a number of different campaigns for my own businesses and those of my clients.

Unless you've already built a reputation for yourself, it is inadvisable to quote your company name within the headline of your ad – it's already there in your URL, so don't waste precious word count repeating yourself. It's the sales message that will convince users to click through to your site, not your company or trading name.

Asking the audience

Good ad copy piques the reader's interest. And there's no better way to get someone interested in what you have to say than to ask them a question that you already know the answer to.

In the case of a franchise business or an opportunity for home-workers – be it part-time, full-time or casual – then money talks. Without using wild and ridiculous claims of instant wealth, ask away: 'Want to earn £50 an hour at your computer?' That's good money, whatever industry you work in ... tell me how! If I were looking for an opportunity, I'd most certainly click on that question because the answer is most certainly 'yes'. However, conversely, I wouldn't click on an ad that asked 'Want to make £5,000 a day?' because unless the role involved selling copious amounts of cocaine, bank robberies or was just a downright lie, it isn't going to happen – and I'm not even going to click to find out the 'secret'.

Asking questions can work for any industry: 'Looking for an honest estate agent?', 'Looking for pain-free dental surgery?', 'Want to know all the facts about our second-hand cars?'

Instructions can work too: 'Create your will in just five simple steps'; 'Sign up now for a homeowner's loan'. Say what it is you want the user to do and call them to action.

To price or not to price ...

Adding prices to your ad can work for and against you. I have and will continue to use ads that include prices for some products and avoid pricing altogether for other products. It depends on a number of factors, not least whether your prices are cheaper than the competition, whether your competition is quoting prices and whether the product or service you are selling is driven by price.

As with all of this advice, try it and see for yourself. Only you will know for sure whether it works for your ads in your industry for your keywords.

As a rule of thumb, if I am far cheaper than the competition then I'll sing and dance about my pricing. If my prices are similar (or higher) then I'll push other features or benefits of my service and leave it up to the customer to decide whether they want to click through.

Being the cheapest will not always guarantee you the click through. As consumers we are driven by a number of factors and quite often price is not the most important.

Describe, as best you can

Yes your ad is a sales tool. As much as you want to add as many 'power' words and audience grabbers as possible, your ad's primary purpose is to attract users to a specific product or service. As much as your marketing instinct is crying out for you to include 'Free shipping', 'No obligation quote' and 'Free download', have you first successfully conveyed what it is you do? I won't know if I want free shipping if I don't know what it is you're selling!

If your competition is hammering home power words within their ad, yours will stand out if it doesn't. That's more room to spend making it absolutely clear that this ad is for this product.

Writing Tips

We all have a unique writing style (although my editor would argue that my writing style is not so much unique as just plain wrong) and nuances with grammar and punctuation. The good news is that these nuances can be the difference between a successful ad and a mediocre ad. When word count can translate into cash, every single comma, full stop and everyone's favourite, the semi-colon, play a vital role in your advert. Play around with punctuation the same way you do with words. I sometimes end an ad message with three dots … I'm hoping readers understand this to mean 'there's more' and click through accordingly. Although it might be correct to use a comma, use a hyphen instead, or even a double hyphen.

■ If you can be specific in your ad, then do so. 'Increase your efficiency by 25%' looks pretty impressive; I wonder if I'll click through to find out more?

- If there's the opportunity to endorse, do so – Winner WhatCar 2008 – but only if it's true!
- The words 'New', 'Improved' and 'Free' tend to be crowd-pleasers, but again only if it's true and relevant – you might fool users into clicking through, but if they're not buying from you, you're just wasting your money.
- It won't stop everyone from clicking through, but if it's applicable say: 'For women only', 'Only for men', 'Over 18s only'.
- If you're concerned about space, it's acceptable to use an ampersand (&) instead of 'and' – that's two more characters for you to play with.

Again, these tips have been learned through trial and error over a number of years of AdWord campaigns. Without doubt, though, it is important to capitalise every word in your ad (except for 'in', 'on', 'and', etc.).

So, regardless of your headline, an ad saying the following:

Great selection, fast service and
free shipping worldwide

becomes:

> Great Selection – Fast Service
> Free Shipping Worldwide

It's far more eye-catching and more likely to get you that click-through.

Never before has spelling and grammar been so important. Yes, there is some room for manoeuvre in terms of using & instead of 'and' and experimenting with a dash instead of a comma or semi-colon, but there is absolutely no room for error in terms of spelling and knowing when to use the plural or an apostrophe. There are some shocking ads on display with errors to make you wince. Admittedly some people must be clicking on them – otherwise they wouldn't last too long – but how much more effective could they be if the ad writer knew when to use the word babies or baby's, for instance?

I write for a living, but I still make mistakes – we all do – so I have an editor. The same should be true for you and your ads. Have someone check them over for glaring errors – it's not an admission of failure or incompetence; it's common sense. Your business is at stake, and if you're really embarrassed about it you could always just ask for their opinion on which ad they think is going to be the most successful – having read through the selection, they'll hedge their bets and point out ever-so-politely that you've mixed 'their' with 'there' ... again.

Lastly, be sure to target your audience with the language they want to read – quite simply if you're trying to attract consumers, tailor your ad to them; if you're trying to attract businesses, the copy must be different. Consumers generally buy just one of anything whereas businesses will often buy in bulk. You can deter the wrong sort of user or appeal to the right sort of user simply by including the quantities you sell in within the ad. The phrase 'Free delivery on bulk orders' tells me you're selling to the trade, no matter what the product is or what else you've written in your ad. Then, if I'm a business, I might click through; if I'm buying for me, I won't.

After the click-through, what then?

Although we can tweak and alter our ad copy until it's near perfect and enjoying click-through rates that would make your competitors weep (if they knew), it all comes down to absolutely nothing if you don't convert those click-through prospects into paying customers. Conversion is king and the only way you're going to convert users into consumers is by making sure the destination URL is optimised not only to receive these potential customers but also to keep them there and make their path to purchase as seamless and painless as possible.

Optimise the language of your destination URL

Language is a beautiful thing. We have dictionaries full of words to choose from and we have always been told to take our time explaining things to others using the written word. Then along came the information super-highway to add to our already busy, no-time-to-stop lifestyles. Net result – web language was born.

Web language is short, less formal and at times quite chatty, but this does not mean to say that the basic rules of grammar and spelling are any less important – it just means that you can bend the rules occasionally. There is no excuse for mistakes, but you can be clever with your copy and users will be extremely forgiving (and grateful) if you can inject a bit of humour in your web pages.

Sound bites

No matter how well crafted each word of text is on any given web page, only a small percentage of it will actually be read. We, the users, will scan quickly hoping that our eye catches something related to what it is that drove us to this page in the first place. It has to be very well written copy indeed to first gain our attention and then to make us change our instinct from moving on to reading on.

Keep your text short, snappy and focused. Make reference to the keywords you used to entice them to click on your ad – if all the references to what's brought them this far peter out, they'll abandon your site.

Observe your competitors' sites shamelessly. Are they doing something that is different or doing something that is better. If they are funny, make your text funnier. If their site is a little bit tongue-in-cheek compete with wit and take the war of words to them.

Stop jabbering

As a rule of thumb, try not to use more than three paragraphs to describe a product or service. Paraphrasing the old maxim about presentations – tell them what it is, tell them again and then remind them what they've just read. Be economical with your words but reinforce the keyword/s that will help sell. By all means allow users to find out more, such as technical specifications, testimonials, related products etc., but don't let this get in the way of the synopsis. Offer this additional information in the form of links to other pages on your site. Users like to know that there is more information available, should they wish to follow the links, but often just that knowledge often acts as a substitute for actually reading it. The trick is to have information to hand, but for it not to be fighting for space with the sound bite.

Don't be shy about what you have to offer – you've enticed the user to click through to this specific page, now work on them. Be proud, be daring and give them a bit of cleavage to whet their appetites. Bearing in mind that you only have about 10 seconds to hook your user, make it good.

Up and to the front

No matter how much or how little content you have on the destination URL, the key to using space effectively is to *push it up and to the front*. The simple rule is to push the most appealing or important products or articles to the top of the page with everything else forming a frame. This should of course be the product or service around which your AdWord ad was tailored. These words or images or products are your best assets – your family jewels – and they must be promoted and supported. Bearing in mind that most users will not scroll to the bottom of the page – ever – what is above the fold (and therefore will be seen the most) must entice, tease and fulfil your visitors' curiosity enough for them to read on or to make a purchase.

7

Ad testing, tracking and converting

Taking stock

We all have our own ways of writing sales messages. Certainly within the constraints of the tight character count on AdWords, good ad writing really is a fine art. Different messages and styles work for different industries and only by testing your ads will you know what works for your business.

So, you've established a campaign and it's been running now for at least a couple of months. You've got real data to work from and you'll also have a better feel now of what AdWords are and what they can do for your business. Every eight weeks or so, I'd advise running a sort of campaign health check. Here's what you should review.

Automatically Optimise Ad Serving: This is a superb feature, except of course if you are testing new or altered ads. Google allows you to rotate ads evenly to split test one against the other. It also offers to automatically optimise your ads by serving up your best-performing ads more frequently. However, when you're testing a number of ads and you want to identify the best performer, you must turn off the automatic ad optimiser to ensure each version of the ad is displayed evenly. Otherwise, the ad that first shows promise is optimised and shown more, which means the exercise becomes self-fulfilling and you'll never know the true strength of the other n versions…

Naming Convention: When you start your first AdWords ad, it's difficult to know where you are going next and how many ad groups you're going to end up with. Personally, I always call the first campaign 'Campaign number 1' – not original, not very exciting, but it works. Now you've got a number of ads running, it's a good time to start using a convention. Be logical, because one day you're going to want to go on holiday and you'll have to leave your account in the hands of someone else (aargh!!). Will they be able to understand the ads? No, I didn't think so. Name your babies with care!

Settings: Often, when first creating an AdWords campaign, we leave most of the default settings as they are in a rush to get our ad out there and working. But the defaults don't work for everyone, especially in terms of distribution options, language, country and regions. Do you still find the ads served on Google's 'search network' and 'content network' are working for you? (Did you even know you were signed up to them!?) Review, and make a decision to drop or keep them. Likewise, is it time to add or delete countries and/or regions? If there's dead wood, chop it out. If you've conquered the UK, move on to Europe or the US, providing they're applicable to your product or service.

Keyword Refreshment: Maybe your ads are working well with the keywords you've chosen, but remember to use this review time to see what's hot and what's not – there may well have a been a huge shift in user behaviour. Keep abreast and make changes if necessary.

Success? In a nutshell, are you getting a return on your investment? How much are you spending a month on AdWords and what does that equate to in sales? Is that acceptable, too low or beyond your wildest dreams? It's unlikely to be beyond your wildest dreams, no matter how well it's performing, so what are you going to do to improve things? That's right: tweak, edit, rewrite and launch another campaign.

If no sale, what? Sometimes, especially in the early days of a new venture or an established company diversifying into a new product line or service, sales aren't the only indicator of whether your AdWords campaign is working for you. What is important to measure is what action your AdWords ad caused. Did the ad bring users to a form that needed completing? If so was it completed? Did your ad bring users to a page that, in turn, had links to other pages on the site or other sites? If so, how many of those links were clicked? What did your user do next? Obviously only some of this information is collected by Google AdWords, so you'll need as much visibility as posssible of what users are doing on your site too. If this is something that's currently lacking, you need to look into it quickly.

Testing protocol

It's very tempting to make huge alterations to your ads, especially if performance has been somewhat lacklustre. Don't. Make only one alteration at a time, and then retest. This can be a simple alteration in the sentence syntax or a change of word. Retest, and if it's still not working, then make another alteration.

Having done this for quite a few years now, I am still amazed at how much more successful an ad can be just by altering a word, or altering the structure of the message. If you make blanket alterations – essentially creating a brand new ad rather than modifying the one you already have – then you'll miss out on the hidden gems you've already created and be forever making alterations without seeing the benefit.

Play with price

AdWords is a constantly changing marketplace – new advertisers join in, old hands give up or lose interest. Hear this: AdWords punishes the complacent and rewards those who embrace change.

Even if an ad is working, don't stop testing variations – not only how the ad looks, feels and reads, but also by altering your bid price and monitoring what effect this has on your CTR. You may notice that your CTR reduces in a direct relationship with a lower bid, but, equally, due to a number of variables, you may notice that the ad actually performs better and yet is costing you less money. How cool is that!?

Whether your CTR goes up or down, your constant experimenting is feeding valuable data into your campaign and before long you'll know exactly what works for your business in your industry.

What about conversion?

Talking to advertisers who use AdWords day in day out, you can sometimes get sucked in to their way of thinking – namely, that CTR is the be-all and end-all. But it's not. It's only half the battle.

Having a great CTR is marvellous, but is it making you money? And, more importantly, have you got the tools in place to measure this? Google's suite of tools in relation to AdWords is impressive and most of the data you need is available at the click of a mouse through one *dashboard*, but please don't forget to utilise (or if you haven't got anything set up, make sure you do) your own stats, user logs and any back-end facilities you have to monitor traffic behaviour on your web pages. What are users doing once they've clicked through to your destination URL? If it's a generic ad pointing to your homepage, are they navigating through the site or are they bouncing (leaving the homepage without delving further into the site)? If you are pointing to a specific page, such as a registration form or a product detail page, are users completing the form or placing the item in their shopping basket, abandoning the site or navigating somewhere else? You have to know the answers to these questions to truly know whether your AdWords campaign is effective.

Set your website targets the same way you would any resource. If the user is navigating away from the destination URL, there is something wrong with the page or the message you're using to draw users in. If users are hitting your homepage and then bouncing, the reality of your site hasn't delivered what the ad promised. Fix these problems. CTR is important, but not if the click-throughs aren't becoming paying customers.

Revise negative keywords, improve your CTR

No matter how well you research your keywords, and even your list of negative keywords pre-campaign, you will still be attracting unwanted clicks. It is only with the data you start receiving that you can see for yourself if your lists are working. Chances are, when you investigate the query strings, you'll notice that there are lots of click-throughs from a certain keyword that isn't converting – add the problem keyword to your negative list.

Be sure to consider whether you want to block these new negative keywords across your entire account or whether to add them to specific ad groups.

Testing your ads

Split testing your ads is often a long (well, actually, it's never ending) and somewhat fickle task, but it is the time you spend testing your ads against each other that will ultimately result in turning a mediocre AdWords experience into a killer campaign. It is the small subtleties of changing a word in the copy here, or adding a negative keyword there, that can improve the CTR of an ad by an entire percentage point, sometimes even more.

Split testing is the art of having very similar ads competing against each other for the same keywords. All the parameters are the same – the target geographic location/s, the price you are bidding, the keywords and, of course, the negative keywords etc. The difference is in the ad copy – a subtle textual difference, which could be one word, or even just the order in which the words are displayed. The result you are looking for, ordinarily, is an increase in the CTR; proof that one ad attracts more users than another.

To initialise a split test, click on 'Create New Ad' and start writing. There is a school of thought that says it's wise to test a number of ad variants simultaneously – the argument being that you'll find your killer ad quicker with, say, four versions competing against each other. This might work for you, but I think this process is called A/B testing for a reason – it's A versus B and once one proves to be the definite winner, you replace the loser with another slightly tweaked ad and the process starts again.

The two (or more) ads you choose to A/B will not be shown at *exactly* the same rate. However, it's pretty much a 50/50 split and once you have about seven days' worth of data, you'll begin to see from the results that one ad is outperforming the other. Now, most of the time the improved performance of one ad over another can be merely one tenth of a percent. But that is still an improvement, and if you can manage to increase your CTR even by one-tenth of a percent every test cycle, you're going to get more click-throughs and hopefully more customers.

When split testing, you should also be looking at the bigger picture – while improving CTR is incredibly important (not least because it means your ad is not disabled and lives on another day), you should also use your split testing to measure any changes to your *conversion ratio* (the number of users who become consumers) and even ultimately your ROI. Although there are numerous factors that will determine whether someone clicking through on your ad ends up buying a product or service from you, it all starts with that click-through and attracting the right user in the first place.

When writing new copy for the competing 'B' ad, don't be tempted to change too much – subtlety is the name of the game. Week 1 could be adding a call to action, week 2 could be modifying the display URL. Too many alterations and you're not A/B testing anymore; you're trying to compare apples with oranges, and, while the 'B' ad might do very well, you still won't know whether you can improve the 'A' ad and the exercise is wasted.

So much testing, so little time ...

Testing new ads, altering copy, split testing 'A' and 'B' ads – it all takes time. I would argue, though, that it's time well spent. But it may be too much for you to handle on your own, especially if you run a small operation and your time and expertise is expected and needed elsewhere. Personally, I love to stay in control of my AdWords campaigns, so that I can react immediately and retire ads that are failing and boost ads that are doing well. But we all have lives outside of marketing and even hard-working folks such as yourselves deserve to take a holiday once in a while rather than melting under the constant weight of the responsibility required to stay ahead of the game.

Help is at hand. And that help is available for what is a nominal fee compared with what a medium-size or large AdWords campaign might be costing you per month. For around $20 a month, there are companies who will take the pain out of testing. Here are two of them:

www.loweryourbidprice.com
http://www.winneralert.com/

Pay their fees, and sit back and wait for the e-mail notifications to come through. All the hard work is done and your 'winning' ads will be highlighted so that you can get on with the next test.

It's worth visiting the WinnerAlert homepage just to read the sales pitch, which is refreshingly funny. Added to that, they give a free 14-day trial.

Measuring conversion

There is a good reason why Google offers you the chance to enter a destination URL and a display URL, and if you find you're entering the same information into both fields, then chances are you are not exploiting your AdWords campaign to its maximum potential. While the display URL should be clear, concise and clutter-free (even if you decide to use it as an opportunity to include a sales message or 'power word'), the destination URL can be anything you like, and the emphasis here is to use it to help you track conversion. Figure 8 shows what I mean.

All I have done here is embed a simple code into the URL so that when the user clicks through to my website – in this case my homepage – I can track their actions through my own back-end software. In this example, the user's visit to my site tells me that the user clicked on an ad from my 'template' keyword group and it was ad variant number 53. Without this code, I wouldn't have a clue which ad had drawn the user to my homepage. Although I would know the referrer was Google AdWords, I wouldn't be able to discern which ad had earned me money.

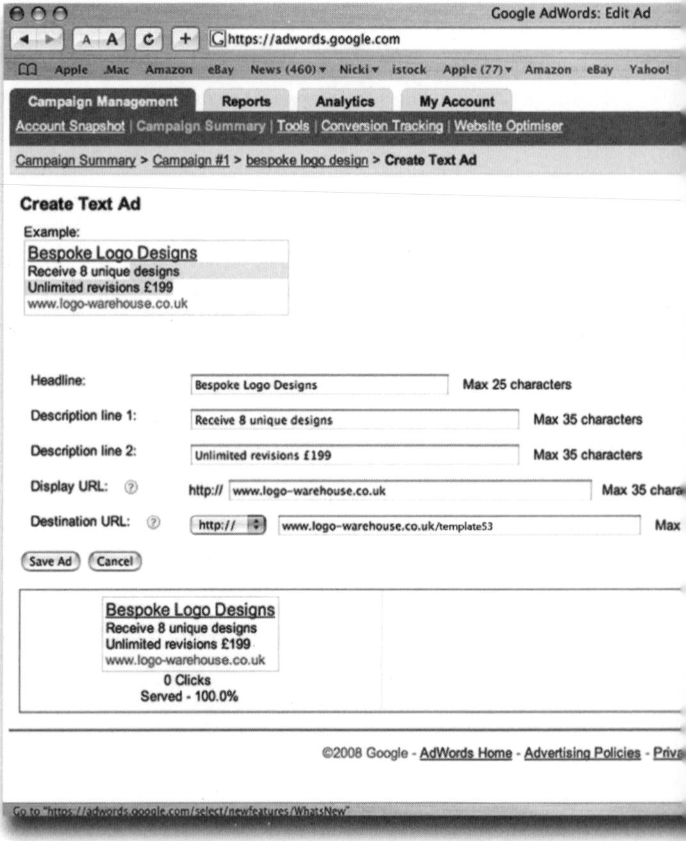
Google AdWords: Edit Ad
https://adwords.google.com
Apple .Mac Amazon eBay News (460) Nicki istock Apple (77) Amazon eBay Yahoo!
Campaign Management
Reports
Analytics
My Account
Account Snapshot | Campaign Summary | Tools | Conversion Tracking | Website Optimiser
Campaign Summary > Campaign #1 > bespoke logo design > Create Text Ad
Create Text Ad
Example:
Bespoke Logo Designs
Receive 8 unique designs
Unlimited revisions £199
www.logo-warehouse.co.uk
Headline:
Bespoke Logo Designs
Max 25 characters
Description line 1:
Receive 8 unique designs
Max 35 characters
Description line 2:
Unlimited revisions £199
Max 35 characters
Display URL:
http://
www.logo-warehouse.co.uk
Destination URL:
http://
www.logo-warehouse.co.uk/template53
Save Ad
Cancel
Bespoke Logo Designs
Receive 8 unique designs
Unlimited revisions £199
www.logo-warehouse.co.uk
0 Clicks
Served - 100.0%
©2008 Google - AdWords Home - Advertising Policies
Go to "https://adwords.google.com/select/newfeatures/WhatsNew"

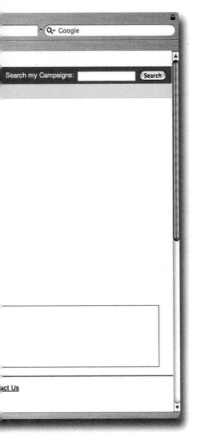

Figure 8 By adding 'template-53' to the destination URL I can track what users clicking on this particular Ad gets upto on my web-site.

By copying this technique across the entire range of ad groups, and with the help of a simple Excel spreadsheet (which is now updated automatically by a data feed from the site's back-end – you've got to love technology!), I receive a daily report on how effective my ads are, not just in terms of CTR but also in terms of conversion – and I can put a financial value on that conversion and decide whether to suspend, edit or even increase my spend on a particular ad or ad group.

Knowing what to measure

When embarking on your Google AdWords campaign, your primary goal is, of course, to achieve a healthy click-through rate. It is this CTR that will ultimately decide whether Google will allow your ad to continue, or whether it will be disabled. It is also the click-through rate that measures how effective your ad is with the general search public and, ultimately, if they're clicking on your ad, you're doing something right – whether they then become customers depends on how good a job your website does in converting them.

Remember, though, that the CTR is not everything. Yes, it will remain in the background as a critical yardstick to measure performance, but as you embark on your Google AdWords experience, it is paramount that you and the other stakeholders in your business know exactly what it is you wish to achieve from Google AdWords. If your main goal is to drive traffic from Google or its partners to your site – where, ultimately, the user will buy at least one product or service from you, there and then – that's great and relatively straightforward. It could also be that you want to use Google AdWords to promote a certain aspect of your business, such as one of the many services you offer or a certain product range (be it low or high value), that you feel will benefit from online advertising. In addition, most businesses, although they want instant sales, should be using Google AdWords for a number of other reasons too. Brand awareness is still an important part of the marketing mix and AdWords can help you achieve this. Bringing down the cost per acquisition, compared with traditional or offline-marketing efforts, is another.

Whatever your goals, do not lose sight of them. Utilising Google AdWords is hard work, time consuming and there are no shortcuts or viable ways to avoid having to do the research or the constant monitoring. However, when AdWords works, it works well and it's easy to get caught up in the excitement of a successful campaign – but, then, how do you measure success? Is is CTR? Is it ROI? Is it brand awareness and company exposure? Is it the cost of new customer acquisition? I think it's all of these things combined and that means you need to be looking at all of these measurables closely.

From user to consumer – the customer's journey

In chapter 6 we looked at the importance of great ad copy leading to a high click-through rate, which in turn leads users to your destination URL. But, to truly convert, your user must do more than read copy on your website; they must interact – and hopefully that interaction means calling you, completing a form or ordering a product. How easy is that process on your site?

Successful businesses on the Internet are not just made by driving thousands or millions of people to your site – that bit, if you have a strong enough offering (or buckets of cash to spend on AdWords) is relatively easy. The trick is to convert your users into consumers and ensure that when they leave, some of their money has been left with you ...

Your site is not there to look pretty; it's there for a reason – to make money. Unashamedly pimp your site and don't let your working pages go to sleep on the job, so to speak. Keep tweaking your webpages; keep improving your offering.

The road to Damascus

A great way to try to understand why not every visitor ends up buying products or downloading information from your site is to focus on how you behave when surfing the Internet. Not every single user on your website will consume – and there is nothing you can do about that fact. But with the average conversion ratio of anything between 1% and 5%, how can you ensure that you are at the top rather than the bottom of this scale (or even on it)? Firstly, there are going to be visitors to your site who really are *just looking*, for whatever reason – your ad just made them aware of your existence. Secondly, there are visitors who found you by complete accident and don't know where they are going, or why they are here – they simply saw your ad and loved the message so much, they clicked. Some will scan your destination URL and leave immediately (bouncers) while others will have a quick read because something in the ad caught their eye, but they won't become consumers. When you visit a website what dictates whether you end up buying? Well, a number of factors come into play ...

Big brand, little brand

Brand awareness will eventually happen over time, through trust (maybe because of a parent company or sympathetic PR) or because it is bought through a massive advertising campaign with a budget that would leave most of us aghast. Branding does take time, but once your brand is established it will help users become consumers just by virtue of who you are. Everything might be right about your site – the look, the feel, the navigation and the price of your products or services – but Joe Bloggs hasn't heard of you before and, certainly when you are selling products that cost any more than £25, becomes reluctant to part with his cash for no better reason than you're not familiar enough ... yet.

Giving it up

A major complaint from users, when they are not chasing their orders, refers to a lack of information available on the website. Now, although it is important to keep web copy short, snappy and to a minimum, there is no excuse for not including the basic information about the products you are expecting your users to actually spend money on. If your ad has attracted the user to click through, their experience on your site must be perfect. Users want more information – about the product, about the service, about the meaning of life. If you don't provide the information necessary to make users comfortable enough to purchase, then they'll be off to another site where the information is more freely available – net result: lost business and lost revenue. And all this for not repeating verbatim what has been provided to you by the manufacturer or supplier, or your own sales documentation ... very poor indeed.

Where exactly am I?

Users will feel a lot happier about spending time on your site and committing to spending some money if they can actually get around the site in a logical manner. It's paramount to ensure that you have good navigation, with links and buttons that not only work, but also take users quickly and seamlessly to exactly where they want to go. Improve your site navigation and you will see a rise in your conversion ratio.

Your destination URL worked but, once a user continues on their journey within your site, or orders and embarks along the order pipeline, then the pages have to maintain the quality and integrity the customer has already come to expect.

The order pipeline

The buying process itself can scare a lot of users away, even though up until that moment you had them hooked on you, your pricing and your products. It beggars belief that websites spend all of their time and effort (and, it would appear, cash) on designing the ultimate site in terms of attractive navigation and well-presented products, but then let themselves down, spectacularly, with the final and most important step – the shopping basket and order pipeline. As much time and effort should go into the design and implementation of the order pipeline as went into the look and feel of your homepage. Getting users to select products or services from your site and put them into a basket or cart is only half the battle – you now need to get them to walk through the checkout without abandoning the purchase.

Despite the best efforts of your AdWords campaign to attract new visitors to the site, the efforts of merchandising to ensure the right products are available at the right price, and the efforts of the sales/editorial department to present the products in the best possible light, if it all goes wrong at the end and users find it difficult to actually buy from you, then it is all in vain. Make the ordering process problem-free for the customer and don't let them leave without spending some money!

The process of users placing items into their shopping baskets and their subsequent path to purchase is often referred to as the order pipeline. This is the distance and number of pages a consumer must face before their choice/s of purchase become their own. Just as good web design is all about offering both simplicity and usability, an effective order pipeline must be equally short and to the point. If you had to complete an obstacle course every time you wanted to conduct your weekly grocery shop, you would soon look to another supermarket that was far easier to navigate and give them your custom. The same is true for websites.

Just the basics, please

When designing or redesigning your order pipeline, look to shave off as many stages as possible between a user selecting what they want to buy and the order confirmation page. You need to look at your current set-up and define what details are important for this order and what can be captured at a later date. If you have the time and the tools, look at how many customers place an item in their basket and how many complete their order. The lost custom is absolutely heartbreaking. You will be losing about 50% of your custom for every page of the order pipeline. So, if one hundred people put an item into their baskets and there are five pages of order pipeline, you will be looking at just over three orders actually being completed. Imagine the difference if you take away two of those pages – you will be enjoying over twelve orders per one hundred instead of just three.

Keep them informed

Even after perfecting your order pipeline, there are some delays that you simply cannot eradicate and the main culprit is when the website is trying to confirm with your bank that the customer's card details are legitimate. Although you cannot speed this process up, you can let your consumers know what is going on. Even if it is as simple as showing a sand timer or a message, make it clear that the site is still working and it's just looking for information from another source.

Likewise it is probably worth your while to offer a phone number and a fax number for people wanting to leave their credit card details. Although the fear has gone from most web users about the safety of their card details, there still exist some users who feel safer reading their card number to a human being rather than entering the details online. You are quite within your rights to charge a surcharge to cover the associated administration costs. Having someone man the phones for users who are having difficulty ordering from you will most certainly give you a good ROI; letting your users abandon their baskets will not.

One eye on the future

Sadly, at time of writing, the technology is only in beta form, but from what I can gather, 'click to play' video advertising is coming … and it has so many possibilities. Video Advertising (currently only available through Google's Content Network) is going to make AdWords truly Web 2.0 – that is, the displaying of information, on demand, in a truly multimedia way. AdWords will still be displayed as text only ads, but there will be an option (and it will very much be opt-in to keep within the principles of Google's 'less is more' business ethic) to see video ads alongside, or instead of, the text ad. Imagine the possibilities – a twenty second, movie-style 'trailer' showing your product in action, or walking users through the registration process.

Why will it work? Well, we already see that Google's acquisition of YouTube in 2006 is evolving a new form of text-based advertising that will appear on a mutually relevant YouTube page. But what about search-based TV-commercial-quality video advertising that is *pulled* onto a potential customer's screen based on a product or relevant search query? Let's first quickly look at what's wrong with traditional TV commercial advertising to give you an idea of where AdWords could possibly be headed. For starters, advertisers can't be sure of who is watching their advert. TV commercial creation and broadcast costs are prohibitive to all but a few major brands. The advert is *pushed* onto the screen and not requested by the viewer. There are now so many TV channels to choose from, fragmenting an already shrinking viewing audience. There is no way to prove the financial success of your television advertising campaign with any accuracy – and, of course, there now exists hardware that allows the viewer to 'skip' the advertising altogether. Not as compelling a marketing tool as it once seemed, then?!

Traditional TV advertising's loss, however, is to become AdWords' gain. The AdWords system of advert delivery solves all of the above problems, so if you could combine the instant audio-visual impact of a TV campaign with the ruthless efficiency of AdWords, you would have a highly effective business development tool at your disposal. A fantastic new era is emerging for all AdWords advertisers to run their own highly affordable, professionally created TV commercials through an AdWords account.

The potential is massive and at the moment there only seems to be one serious service provider in the UK ready to harness this new dawn of video pay per click (PPC) marketing.

www.admoogle.tv/

Take a look and use them if it appeals.

A word of warning...

If you've created a campaign and it's working really well for you, that's great. I'm all for a bit of back-slapping. In fact, when working for US companies, I've even been known to join in with the occasional 'whoop' every now and again. Yes, success is brilliant, but don't rest on your laurels, not even for a week. AdWords campaigns work – you've seen that now with your own eyes in relation to your own site – but there are always competitors waiting to leap into your position. Rest assured that as more and more users become familiar with AdWords and realise the importance of testing, measuring and tweaking, they'll be nipping at your ankles from now on.

Stay ahead of the game. Continue to test, continue to run new ads and constantly strive to improve your ROI. You can never refine too much. Yes, you'll take some wrong turns along the way, but you'll know how to revert back to your successful form again.

Survivors adapt; those who remain static perish.

Good luck!

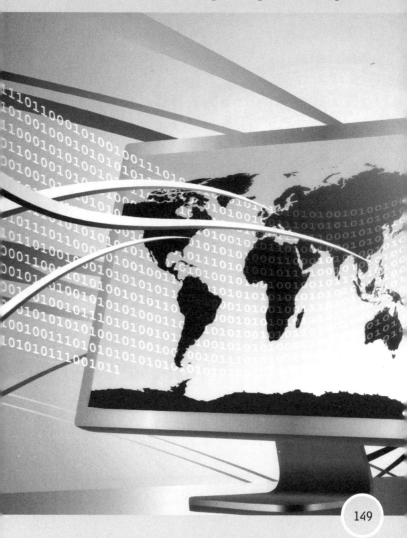

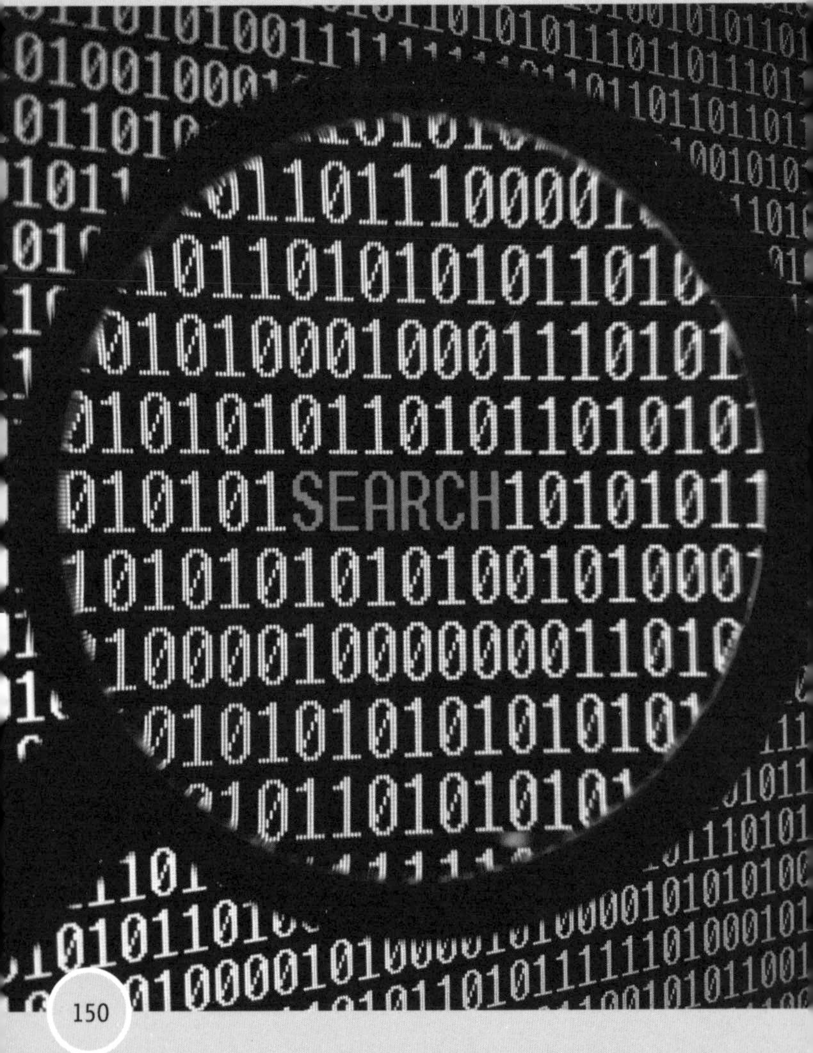
SEARCH

Index

If you enjoyed this book, you may also like...

Get into bed with Google

Top ranking search optimisation techniques

Sleep your way to the top of search engine
rankings by learning the secret tips and
techniques needed to achieve the best
search engine optimisation for your web site.

SAVE 30%* – buy for only
£6.99 [rrp £9.99]

Podcasting

The ultimate starter kit

A light-hearted, friendly, and refreshingly
jargon-free look at everything you need
to know to start podcasting.

SAVE 38%* buy for only
£4.99 [rrp £7.99]

For full details of these books and others in the 52 Brilliant Ideas series
please visit www.infideas.com.

*Offer is good until you decide to use this book as a door stop.

How to place your order

Qty	Title	RRP
	Get into bed with Google	£6.99
	Podcasting	£4.99
	Subtotal	
	Postage (see below)	
	TOTAL	

Name: ....

Delivery address: ....

....

....

E-mail:................................Tel (in case of problems):...........................

(We never give details to 3rd parties nor will we bombard you with lots of junk mail!)

By post

Fill in all the relevant details, cut this page out and send along with a cheque made payable to Infinite Ideas.
Send to: Infinite Ideas, 36 St Giles, Oxford OX1 3LD, UK

infinite ideas

Credit card orders over the telephone

Call +44 (0) 1865 514 888. Please quote reference GOOGLEAD08.

Any questions please call +44 (0) 1865 514 888 or e-mail info@infideas.com.

Postage and packaging rates: UK: £2.49, EU: £5, RoW: £8